**New Directions for
Institutional Research**

Robert K. Toutkoushian
EDITOR-IN-CHIEF

J. Fredericks Volkwein
ASSOCIATE EDITOR

Data Mining
in Action:
Case Studies
of Enrollment
Management

Jing Luan
Chun-Mei Zhao
EDITORS

Number 131 • Fall 2006
Jossey-Bass
San Francisco

DATA MINING IN ACTION: CASE STUDIES OF ENROLLMENT MANAGEMENT
Jing Luan, Chun-Mei Zhao (eds.)
New Directions for Institutional Research, no. 131
Robert K. Toutkoushian, Editor-in-Chief

NEW DIRECTIONS FOR INSTITUTIONAL RESEARCH (ISSN 0271-0579, electronic ISSN 1536-075X) is part of The Jossey-Bass Higher and Adult Education Series and is published quarterly by Wiley Subscription Services, Inc., A Wiley Company, at Jossey-Bass, 989 Market Street, San Francisco, California 94103-1741 (publication number USPS 098-830). Periodicals Postage Paid at San Francisco, California, and at additional mailing offices. POSTMASTER: Send address changes to New Directions for Institutional Research, Jossey-Bass, 989 Market Street, San Francisco, California 94103-1741.

SUBSCRIPTIONS cost $80.00 for individuals and $185.00 for institutions, agencies, and libraries. See order form at end of book.

EDITORIAL CORRESPONDENCE should be sent to Robert K. Toutkoushian, Educational Leadership and Policy Studies, Education 4220, 201 N. Rose Ave., Indiana University, Bloomington, IN 47405.

New Directions for Institutional Research is indexed in *College Student Personnel Abstracts, Contents Pages in Education,* and *Current Index to Journals in Education* (ERIC).

Microfilm copies of issues and chapters are available in 16mm and 35mm, as well as microfiche in 105mm, through University Microfims, Inc., 300 North Zeeb Road, Ann Arbor, Michigan 48106-1346.

www.josseybass.com

THE ASSOCIATION FOR INSTITUTIONAL RESEARCH was created in 1966 to benefit, assist, and advance research leading to improved understanding, planning, and operation of institutions of higher education. Publication policy is set by its Publications Committee.

For information about the Association for Institutional Research, write to the following address:

AIR Executive Office
114 Stone Building
Florida State University
Tallahassee, FL 32306-4462

(850) 644-4470

air@mailer.fsu.edu
http://airweb.org

CONTENTS

EDITORS' NOTES

By its nature, the *New Directions for Institutional Research* series tackles some of the most challenging practices and introduces exciting emerging technologies. In this volume, the coeditors collected and showcased the application of data mining for enrollment management. What better way to introduce a new, difficult, and sometimes misconstrued concept like data mining than by showing how it works on the timely subject of enrollment management in solving real-life problems?

Data mining continues to be loosely defined, and different people have different understandings of what it is. But data mining, just like its popular counterpart, traditional statistics, is a way of analyzing and examining data to uncover hidden information. Data-mining processes invoke fancy terminologies and exotic algorithms that seem elusive to many serious minds trained in traditional statistical applications.

The digital age and the vastly expanding capacity of computing power and data collection and storage have handed the institutional research community a tremendous opportunity to look at data in a new light, to provide more ways of analyzing and extracting quality information from data. In some sense, it is imperative that new ways be explored and utilized to handle the ever-expanding data warehouses!

Misconceptions about and resistance to data mining persist despite its being widely utilized in marketing, medicine, banking, insurance, and even criminology (Westphal and Blaxton, 1998; Thearling and others, 2004). The institutional research community has a love affair with the traditional statistical rules of hypothesis testing, universe sampling, significance-level estimation parameters, and so forth. A significant p value or a high R^2 value brings a sense of serenity to most researchers.

Institutional research is also a practical or action-oriented field. Practitioners do not usually have the luxury of conducting a true experimental study and, thus, to adequately test hypotheses and compare group means. Two serious problems face institutional research. The first is the heterogeneity among students, which translates into how to address individual differences and take correspondent actions. The second is the intrinsic conflict of traditional statistics and the institutional research reality: that is, the emphasis on true experimental research and randomly

The following individuals have provided invaluable time, resources, and support: Judy Cassada, Cabrillo College; Thulasi Kumar, University of Northern Iowa; Brian Leath, Nektar; Mark Rodeghier, University of Chicago; and Robert Valencic, SPSS, Inc.

NEW DIRECTIONS FOR INSTITUTIONAL RESEARCH, no. 131, Fall 2006 © Wiley Periodicals, Inc.
Published online in Wiley InterScience (www.interscience.wiley.com) • DOI: 10.1002/ir.183

selected representative samples versus the presence of large, universal data sets. These can be cumbersome and "messy" and, in real-time data mining, the data are ever-changing.

Many researchers have already made bold moves in unshackling themselves from this quandary. In recent years, there has been a growing effort to apply data mining to solve traditional institutional research problems (Byers Gonzalez and DesJardins, 2002; Luan, 2001, 2003; Luan, Zhao, and Hayek, 2004; Serban and Luan, 2002; Thomas and Galambos, 2004). This led the coeditors to take on the challenge of introducing the tough subject of data mining through real-life examples of enrollment management.

In this volume, we first revisit and redefine the concept of data mining, its use in institutional research, myths about data mining, and differences between traditional statistical analysis and data-mining applications. Then six case studies from universities and colleges are provided to illustrate and examine how data mining works and can be applied to solve day-to-day problems and to inform and enhance institutional decision making. These case studies cover a broad spectrum of research methods and issues, all in the realm of enrollment management. Enrollment management is critical to an institution. It is also an institution-wide process that embraces virtually every aspect of an institution's function and culture. The case studies include topics of admission yields, student retention, and degree-completion time, to name a few. These case studies explore questions such as discovering which inquiries are most likely to turn into actual applications; predicting enrollment to specific courses to help determine a program's success rate; identifying and targeting students who are at risk of attrition; and achieving and maintaining optimum graduation rates, recruitment, and retention rates. Data used in the case studies include both cross-sectional and longitudinal data. Each case study is a chapter by itself.

In Chapter One, we provide a detailed comparison between data mining and traditional statistics, two different approaches to understanding data, each complementing the other. Statistics is an integral component in data mining. As a matter of fact, a few basic elements of traditional statistics deserve continued attention in the data-mining process: data preparation and data cleansing, variable selection, and contextual knowledge.

The explorative nature of data mining and the hypothesis-based approach of traditional statistics are discussed. Further, the cornerstone notion of data mining examines individuals and their behaviors, whereas traditional statistics focuses on group differences.

In Chapter Two, Serge Herzog estimates student retention and degree-completion time. The prediction accuracy of decision trees and artificial neural networks compared with that of logistic regression yields insights into the potential advantage of data-mining techniques over traditional statistics. Focusing on student retention and time to degree completion, the study illustrates how institutional researchers may benefit from the power of predictive analysis associated with data-mining tools.

NEW DIRECTIONS FOR INSTITUTIONAL RESEARCH • DOI: 10.1002/ir

In the era of renewed interest in enrollment management, reducing high attrition rates is a desired goal for higher education institutions. Yet, data from single-institution databases have so far failed to explain students' transfer-out behavior. Sutee Sujitparapitaya (Chapter Three) examines student mobility in retention outcomes. Typical research studies have focused on a binary outcome variable for attrition, but increasingly, knowledge enhanced by the expanding of data sets indicates that there are at least three possible outcomes: stop-outs, retention, and transfer-outs. This case study represents an initial attempt by a university to employ data-mining techniques to study a ternary attrition variable produced by integrating multiple internal and external databases. This effort has proved to be desirable and effective.

Informed knowledge of a higher education institution's enrollment pattern is essential to design efficient and effective enrollment strategies. Lin Chang (Chapter Four) applied data mining to study admissions yield. In this study, data-mining technology's predictive modeling was applied to enhance the prediction of enrollment behaviors of admitted applicants at a large state university. Admissions data were explored to answer the following questions: (1) Do admitted applicants enroll randomly—that is, no significant patterns existing from one year to another? (2) Are certain types or groups of admitted applicants more likely than others to enroll so that future enrollment can be more accurately predicted? Data-mining modeling processes using Clementine (a proprietary data mining software program developed by SPSS, Inc.) were adopted and evaluated in comparison.

Christopher M. Antons and Elliot N. Maltz illustrate a case study in Chapter Five that utilized data mining to expand the role of institutional research at small private universities. Private college revenues rely heavily on tuition income. Therefore, effective prediction of the expected yield of admitted students is vital to successful fiscal planning. At institutions where institutional research departments have limited staff and resources, the task of projecting yield is often outsourced. This can result in a significant loss of control of the enrollment management process and subsequent shortfalls in tuition revenue. This case study documents a successful application of data-mining techniques in enrollment management through a partnership between the admissions office, a master's degree program in business administration, and the institutional research office at Willamette University in Salem, Oregon. Such an effort not only created a flexible enrollment management tool that could be effectively leveraged by both admissions personnel and institutional research in-house but enabled the achievement of both enrollment and revenue goals.

Paul W. Eykamp explores which students used advanced-placement units to reduce their time to degree completion in Chapter Six. The conventional wisdom is that undergraduates carrying advanced-placement units tend to have a shortened time to degree. The author explores how data mining can help examine how the lengths of student enrollment are associated with a varying number of advanced-placement units. Multiple approaches, including traditional linear regression, decision tree, neural network, cluster analysis, factor analysis, and backward-looking group identification, were tested and evaluated.

In Chapter Seven, Brenda Arndt Bailey showed how to use data mining to explain Integrated Postsecondary Education Data Systems (IPEDS) graduation rates. Predicted graduation rates provide meaningful contextual information in addition to the actual graduation rate in institutional comparison and benchmarking. Therefore, both actual and predicted graduation rates should be used in IPEDS-based research and institutional planning. The author describes data mining of IPEDS data to develop models that calculate predicted graduation rates for two- and four-year institutions. Different from most data-mining tasks whose unit of analysis is individual student records, this case study is based on aggregated institutional data.

In the final chapter, Chapter Eight, we summarize and integrate the common theme that runs through these case studies to propose a modern mindset for data mining as well as concrete suggestions to institutional practitioners and the Association of Institutional Research as a whole. Last, we demystify data mining and validate the applicability of this technique to research in higher education.

Although differing in inquiries and issues, these case studies share common themes. Most of the studies pooled data from a variety of data sources; one (Chapter Five) involved deliberate collaboration from several departments. Most of the case studies address the linkage of data mining and statistics by exploring both approaches and comparing the results. Most of the case studies demonstrated data mining's superior prediction capability and its scoring function to render individualized treatment to students. The data-mining case studies do not use hypothesis testing or analysis of levels of significance; rather, they employ a data-validation technique by splitting the data files into two random sets and validating the model using a fresh set of mirrored data.

Data mining provides a opportunity to gain new insight and knowledge about data. With the sets of case studies, it is our goal that this volume will furnish a tangible sense of what it entails to conduct data mining. If agreement develops about the significance of its practical application, data mining could become a great contribution to the institutional research field, especially enrollment management.

Jing Luan
Chun-Mei Zhao
Editors

References

Byers Gonzalez, J., and DesJardins, S. "Artificial Neural Networks: A New Approach to Predicting Application Behavior." *Research in Higher Education,* 2002, *43*(2), 235–258.

Luan, J. "Data Mining as Driven by Knowledge Management in Higher Education." Keynote speech at the University of California–San Francisco's SPSS Public Roadshow, 2001.

Luan, J. "Developing Learner Concentric Learning Outcome Typologies Using Clustering and Decision Trees of Data Mining (The OIndex report)." Paper presented at the 43rd Association for Institutional Research Forum, Tampa, Fla., 2003.

Luan, J., Zhao, C., and Hayek, J. "Exploring a New Frontier in Higher Education Research: Using Data Mining Techniques to Create an Institutional Typology." Paper presented at the California Association for Institutional Research Conference, Anaheim, Calif., 2004.

Serban, A. M., and Luan, J. (eds.). *Knowledge Management: Building a Competitive Advantage in Higher Education.* New Directions for Institutional Research, no. 113. San Francisco: Jossey-Bass, 2002.

Thearling K., and others. "Visualizing Data Mining Models." Business Intelligence Knowledge Base: White Papers. 2004. http://businessintelligence.ittoolbox.com/white-papers/visualizing-data-mining-models2718. Accessed July 3, 2006.

Thomas, E., and Galambos, N. "What Satisfies Students? Mining Students' Opinion Data with Regression and Decision Tree Analysis." *Research in Higher Education,* 2004, 45(3), 251–269.

Westphal, C., and Blaxton, T. *Data Mining Solutions.* New York: Wiley, 1998.

JING LUAN is vice chancellor of Educational Services and Planning at San Mateo County Community College District in California.

CHUN-MEI ZHAO is research scholar, the Carnegie Foundation for the Advancement of Teaching.

1

The authors provide an overview of data mining, giving special attention to the relationship between data mining and statistics to unravel some misunderstandings about the two techniques.

Data Mining: Going Beyond Traditional Statistics

Chun-Mei Zhao, Jing Luan

Creating a new theory is not like destroying an old barn and erecting a skyscraper in its place. It is rather like climbing a mountain, gaining new and wider views, discovering unexpected connections between our starting point and its rich environment. But the point from which we started out still exists and can be seen, although it appears smaller and forms a tiny part of our broad view gained by the mastery of the obstacles on the adventurous way up.

Albert Einstein

If the latter half of the twentieth century was marked by transition into an information age, the twenty-first century is when the rubber meets the road. Our existing methods and approaches to understanding data, the backbone of information, are being seriously challenged, even threatened, by the ever-more-unrelenting accumulation of data. As the amount of data increases exponentially, higher education is confronting the crisis of information explosion. Our students expect individualized attention in learning. More individualized and refined research is urgently needed to inform institutions' decision making and to enhance student learning.

Institutional data often contain valuable information essential for more in-depth understanding of students and their college experiences. How can we effectively extract quality knowledge from these data to better understand

NEW DIRECTIONS FOR INSTITUTIONAL RESEARCH, no. 131, Fall 2006 © Wiley Periodicals, Inc.
Published online in Wiley InterScience (www.interscience.wiley.com) • DOI: 10.1002/ir.184

college students' needs and behaviors? This has become a critical aspect of the institutional task and the primary focus of institutional researchers.

Statistics and data mining are analytical approaches to uncovering the knowledge residing in data. Traditionally, statistics has been a powerful tool used by institutional researchers. Statistics has a long history. It plays a pervasive role in our daily life as well as in shaping our thinking. Scientists and scholars acknowledge the fact that statistics has been the most successful information science. In comparison, data mining is a newcomer to the world of data analysis mainly credited for the advancement of technologies in computing and data storage. Because the common goal of these two approaches is to retrieve valuable information from data, they bear an essential kinship. Data mining and statistics are intersecting disciplines.

Data mining is a blend of several disciplines, including statistics, machine learning, and artificial intelligence, to name a few. Since its beginning, data mining has elicited mixed reactions in the statistical world. Some people dismiss it as the snake oil of the computing age. For them, data mining has a pejorative connotation somewhat akin to "data fishing" (Hand, Mannila, and Smyth, 2001). A famous quip is "if you torture data long enough, it will confess to anything." In fact, in some graduate training programs, it was taught that data mining was immature and at best to be avoided. The fact that data mining started out as a loosely defined concept has not helped.

On the other hand, for those who have embraced the new approach, data mining is extolled as the "statistical déjà vu" (Kuonen, 2004) and recognized as representing a new paradigm in data analysis. The fact that data mining has made remarkable inroads into the business world and proved to have enhanced business intelligence and overall productivity and efficiency has given definite credibility to the technique. To them, data mining bears great potential in knowledge discovery.

Despite its obvious connection to statistics, data mining, which often employs "exotic" algorithms and seems to be operating mostly in a black box, has produced a fairly high level of discomfort in the statistical community. The major criticism of data mining centers on the lack of theory in the search for the best predictions and, therefore, that too much power is given to the computer. It is directly contradictory to the traditional understanding of data analysis in which statisticians were trained to first contemplate the theory underlying a problem (such as, what would a theory say about how students make decisions about where to attend college?), use the theory to identify variables that should matter (such as family income, tuition, ability, and so on), and then test the theory. Further complicating the situation, as in the case of predictive analysis, even though data mining may yield better predictions, the model used to obtain the predictions cannot easily be related back to theory (Luan, 2005).

This is a legitimate concern that should be addressed before readers delve into the case studies in this book. In this chapter, we provide an overview of data mining and give special attention to the relationship

NEW DIRECTIONS FOR INSTITUTIONAL RESEARCH • DOI: 10.1002/ir

between data mining and statistics, with the intention to unravel some misunderstandings about statistics and data mining. To achieve this goal, we revisit some fundamental philosophical underpinnings of the two data analytical approaches in a parallel manner.

Statistics

Given that statistics are so ingrained in our thinking, it is worthwhile to review some fundamental conditions about it. Statistics is a discipline with ubiquitous application in almost every facet of life as well as scientific inquiry. It addresses one of the most basic of human needs: to understand the world, how it operates in the face of variation and uncertainty, and how to better control future events (Kuonen, 2004). Statistics includes descriptive statistics and inferential statistics, and the latter has been the basis of many modern statistical studies.

Statistics is inductive in nature: the study of a fraction of reality (that is, a sample) extends understanding to a broader population. The fundamental inductive reasoning can be summed up as "an argument that is judged on a continuum from weak to strong. The stronger the argument, the more reason we have to treat the conclusion to be true, assuming the premises are true" (Kelley, 1994, as quoted in Schield, 1999, p. 1). Therefore, to an inductive researcher, hypotheses and theories can only be proved wrong; they cannot be confirmed, no matter how much evidence has been gathered to support a hypothesis (Schield, 1999).

Statistics consists of a range of methods, from dealing with the best ways of collecting data to data analysis and inference techniques. In statistical inquiries, the data are usually collected with particular questions in mind and then analyzed to answer those questions. When data are used to address problems beyond the original purpose for which the data were collected, they may not be properly suited to these problems. Ideally, most statistical work should be based on experimental studies by dealing with firsthand data.

Data Mining

The burgeoning digital and computing technology and the advancing of data capturing and storing capacity provide new opportunities and challenges for data analysis. With more tools, enhanced computing power, and astronomical accumulation of data, researchers are forced to rethink and enhance the ways of examining data and retrieving information. Data mining ascends as a direct result of these developments.

Data mining is designed to uncover interesting, often unexpected, and previously unknown relationships and structures among variables. Data mining is not intended to test well-established relationships or well-known hypotheses. There is usually a serendipitous element in the data-mining process. The discovery is often carried out by an iterative process in which multiple scenarios and possibilities are tried (Luan, 2006). Major tasks performed by data mining include exploratory data analysis, descriptive modeling (including segmentation and clustering), predictive modeling (such as classification and regression), and discovering patterns and rules (for example, detecting outliers and association rules).

Data mining is designed to handle large data sets. The data can be either existing data collected for other purposes, as convenience or opportunity samples (rather than random samples) or even the entire population at study. The data sets data mining deals with are often more "realistic" or "messy" than traditional statistics. Increasingly, data mining performs real-time data analysis directly atop a live data warehouse.

Similarities Between Statistics and Data Mining

Data mining is closely related to statistics in many ways. Both approaches are interested in deciphering data structure. Both are tools invented to tackle uncertainties and inform future events. And both data mining and statistics pay attention to identifying important factors influencing an event and applying the derived model to better predict future events.

Statistics is one of the building blocks of data mining. Statistics provides common vocabularies for describing data. Well-known statistical algorithms such as generalized linear modeling have found their ways into the data-mining tool set. Therefore, data mining is completely capable of conducting traditional statistical analysis. In this sense, data mining can be viewed as an extension and expansion of statistics.

No significant difference exists between data mining and statistics in the common elements essential to a sensible data analysis—that is, data knowledge, background knowledge about how data are collected, measurement issues, design, and fundamental understanding of the context of a practical problem.

Differences Between Statistics and Data Mining

The interrelatedness of data mining and statistics does not disguise the fact that they differ in several fundamental ways, including the role of theory, the generalizability of results, hypothesis testing, and level of significance.

Role of Theory. Statistics has a symbiotic relationship with theory. A theory serves as a searchlight that provides a conceptual framework or an angle for looking into the observations and facts within its realm. Without the guidance of the theory, the sheer amount of observations and facts can be overwhelming. Statistical analysis typically starts with a theory based on previous knowledge and seeks evidence to reject or affirm the theory. Theories in statistics are specific, narrowly defined, with limited alternatives.

Statistics by nature is a confirmatory process. Theory serves as a framework to guide the analyst's attention to make sense of seemingly uncon-

NEW DIRECTIONS FOR INSTITUTIONAL RESEARCH • DOI: 10.1002/ir

nected and scattered facts. However, as a way of seeing, a theory is also a way of not seeing. It runs the risk of generating a "confirmatory bias"—that is, the tendency to believe facts or results that corroborate one's presumptions and ignore those that do not (Mahoney, 1977). As a result, we can become blind to certain facts that do not fall into the searchlight of theory. In this sense, a statistical inference can become a "serendipity-lost" experience.

Data mining, on the other hand, does not focus on theory confirmation. This does not mean that the computer can find the patterns you are looking for or make a prediction automatically. This is one of the common myths about data mining. To the contrary, data mining needs clear directions from the analyst. However, compared with statistics, data mining is less confined in presumptions about the relations among variables, thus leaving ample space for discoveries that might not occur otherwise.

Guided by a theory, traditional statistics is a top-down approach. In contrast, data mining is a bottom-up approach (Mena, 1998). Theory serves as a simplifying mechanism, and the emergence of sample is also a way of reducing computation burden so that, to both save computer time and avoid overextending computer capacity, only a limited number of calculations are conducted. Case in point: it was not until the late 1970s that statistical calculations were no longer carried out by hand. Before the computer revolution, analytical data often existed with limited data capacity. Therefore, statistics is a shortcut, and statisticians need to infer from a sample and apply what might be true to a much larger population. Data mining, equipped with the luxury of computing power, can afford the searching of data patterns in much larger data structures and much more pervasively. Friedman (1997) pointed out that "computing has been one of the most glaring omissions in the set of tools that have so far defined statistics" (p. 5).

The visionary statistician John Tukey foresaw the value of explorative data analysis; as a matter of fact, data mining shares a similar philosophical root with exploratory data analysis, and there are heavy overlaps between exploratory data analysis and data mining. In his 1962 landmark article, "The Future of Data Analysis," Tukey documented his shift in thinking from a statistical point of view to a data analysis point of view—that is, from fixating inferences from the particular to the general to fully recognizing the specificity within the data themselves and a lessened interest in generalization. To illustrate the difference between the two approaches, Tukey pointed out that a statistician works more like a judge examining and testing clearly identified hypotheses, whereas a data analyst is like a detective, open to a wide range of ideas, possibilities, and idiosyncrasies.

If statistics starts and ends with an all-encompassing theory, data mining provides concrete information about how to go about the action. To illustrate, suppose John Smith is a minority student in the first year of college. Data mining asks the question, "Will John Smith return to college for his sophomore year?" A hypothesis-based research question asks, "Are minority students as likely as other students to return to college?"

NEW DIRECTIONS FOR INSTITUTIONAL RESEARCH • DOI: 10.1002/ir

Data mining is not overly concerned about the explanatory power of a model, but rather, focuses on prediction accuracy at an individual level. Therefore, some potentially hazardous issues in statistics, such as multicollinearity (or extremely high correlations among variables), are not a big concern for data mining because data mining is not trying to interpret or isolate the collective causes but rather focuses on each unit of analysis and information presiding in the data that can lead to actionable steps.

A caveat about statistical inference is that despite its claimed explanatory power, in many correlational studies employing traditional statistics, assertions such as that a certain independent variable is the cause of the dependent variable cannot be made. This is because only rigorously controlled experimental studies can conclusively demonstrate causal relationships between variables.

Generalizability. For statistics, the sample itself is seldom the interest of the research. Researchers are interested in the sample only to the extent that it can provide information about the population from which it was drawn. Statistics is not intended to handle individuality. It is designed to find commonalities among subjects.

The aim of data mining is to incorporate more detailed, specific, and local information; it is less ambitious about making a global statement that can be generalized to a much wider population (Luan, 2005). Tukey raised a few provocative thoughts when he pointed out that statisticians should "reject the role of 'guardian of proven truth,' and resist attempts to provide once-for-all solutions and tidy over-unifications of the subject" (summarized by A. Gordon, as quoted by O'Connor and Robertson, 2006).

As a matter of fact, to generate a global model that is useful is an ambitious and even unrealistic task. A model is a simplification of reality, and a global model excludes low-level details, focusing only on a high level of abstraction that summarizes the data structure because it assumes homogeneity within the population. A globally generalizable model usually contains less detailed information than a specific model. But reality is extremely complicated, especially for social sciences, and fraught with difficulties and ambiguities stemming from deficiencies in measurement, design, and analysis.

That is why many statistical models often have low thresholds when the variance of dependent variables is interpreted (for example, it is not uncommon to discover in the literature of social science that the R^2 is less than 0.20). Although a typical statistical regression model uses a few variables to generalize to an entire population, data mining provides the potential to take advantage of information at a more detailed and specific level.

In the business world, one of the major usages of data mining is customer relations management. It was a business ideal to understand each customer individually and his or her idiosyncratic behaviors. Applying it to the educational setting, it is about learner-relationship management, and data mining has great potential to customize student learning experiences and thus induce better educational outcomes (Serban and Luan, 2002).

Hypothesis Testing. Hypothesis testing does not have specific meaning for data mining because data mining does not start from a theory or hypothesis or stress the generalization of results to a specific population. In addition, with data mining, because of its capability in handling a large amount of data, oftentimes the whole population is its study universe. Therefore, the significance level used in statistics for the purpose of estimating the accuracy of inference loses its relevance.

Further, whereas hypothesis testing is the cardinal rule in statistical reasoning and long cherished in the research community, there are practical difficulties and ethical concerns about maintaining test-control groups in a social science setting. Researchers in social sciences often do not have the luxury of conducting a clinical-trial type of analysis. Thus, hypothesis testing in its strictest sense becomes severely limited.

Because of its attention to specificity, data mining is advantageous in providing the individual and granular findings by producing scores for individual subjects or cases. This is more desirable in institutional research work such as enrollment management. In the ensuing chapters, readers will notice that hypothesis testing has not been used in any of the case studies.

Level of Significance. Statistics often lends a "magic touch" to research inquiries because it furnishes a tangible and straightforward criterion: level of significance. Level of significance is a threshold for assessing the defensibility or sustainability of a hypothesis based on a sample. It is a convenient rule-of-thumb index but is often used as the only gatekeeper that safeguards the legitimacy of inference from a sample to a population.

Having a level of significance does not by itself make the research any more scientific. In fact, it may be of limited use. Data are vulnerable to many sources of errors or biases, such as sample selection, measurement, recording, calculation, and so on. The significance level addresses only one of many threats to the validity of a study. As a matter of fact, no statistical tests for sample bias or confounding factors are available.

In addition, being statistically significant does not correlate directly with the practical usage or value of findings. In statistics, the selection of significance level, based on which hypothesis will be rejected as invalid, is arbitrary. Most studies in statistical research choose the conventional significance level (such as a p value of less than .05 or .01) regardless of the nature of the research and subjects in the study. Statistical significance does not automatically imply practical significance. This is especially the case in large data sets, where statistical significance is more easily obtained.

Many statistical research studies commonly present only one sample and proceed to recommend findings based on the single sample. In such cases, there is no way to judge how biased the sample or how valid the data could be. Guttman (1985) pointed out that "the idea of accepting or rejecting a null hypothesis on the basis of a single experiment . . . is antithetical to science" (pp. 4–5). But despite its importance, replications of studies based on different samples are extremely rare in social science practices.

Replication is, however, widely used in data mining. Scientific research requires multiple ways to validate findings. Different algorithms were originally designed for different purposes. As a result, algorithmic biases exist. That is, prediction results differ for a data set produced by multiple algorithms. Some algorithms will naturally work well with some data sets, but not all. Because one test may not fit every data set, several tests should be run on the same data set to observe the confluence and divergence of different algorithms. For example, Willett (2004) studied the differences in results from binary logistic regression and classification and regression tree and noted detectable differences. Herzog notes in Chapter Two the comparative studies of one data-mining algorithm versus another by several scholars.

Data mining also keeps the accuracy of a model in check by splitting the data into a training set and a validation set. The training set of data is used to develop a parsimonious model that maximizes the predictive power of the model; then the model is applied to the validation set to examine the consistency between the two. Having both a training and validation set is of enormous importance. Validation should be an ongoing process as new data accumulate. Data mining does not stop at the stage where the common regression analysis stops—that is, finding out which variables are more important than others; rather, data mining continues on to use all possible permutations of interaction patterns from all variables.

Although statistics emphasizes rigor (often reflected in the level of statistical significance) in inferring theories, data mining seeks advantageous information; even with only a slight advantage, it is better than the alternative. So data mining emphasizes the actionable and practical implications instead of sticking to the absolute rigor that is narrowly defined and operated on in many statistical research studies.

Despite the differences between data mining and statistics, it is critical to keep in mind that they are not contradictory methods. Traditional statistics has a special place in data mining. The basic principles inherent in traditional statistics also deserve close attention in the data-mining process, including a fundamental understanding of the context of the practical problem, of data measurement and data preparation, and so on. Statistical literacy is important for understanding and interpreting data-mining findings. The two approaches should be mutually reinforcing. By joining forces with statistics, data mining can have a powerful effect on knowledge building and discovery. Figure 1.1 displays the role of traditional statistics in a data-mining environment.

Key Features of Data Mining

Potentially an end-to-end tool for data analysis, data mining has several strengths. When one goes beyond the argument over the pros and cons of statistics and data mining, the following features of data mining are attractive to both analysts and decision makers: scalability, streaming on canvas, data accessibility, all-in-one suite, and automation.

New Directions for Institutional Research • DOI: 10.1002/ir

Figure 1.1. The Role of Traditional Statistics in the Entire Data-Mining Process

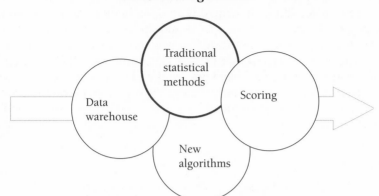

Scalability. In higher education, once the data have accumulated for more than five or ten semesters, the database is a mile deep and just as wide. A data-mining application typically has the ability to accommodate (scale up) this newfound extreme; thus, the researcher can get a handle on what is possibly inside the database in terms of patterns, trends, and factors.

Streaming on Canvas. Most existing tools of data queries are either code based or "point-and-click," and all of them rely excessively on intermediate and isolated tasks. With the introduction of data mining, the process of querying a database has suddenly become workable, with a visual display of the entire flow of data and its transformations.

Data Accessibility. As a prerequisite to successful data analysis, major data-mining programs all have the most accommodating access to data sources: text, flat files, Excel tables, familiar statistical software programs (Statistical Package for the Social Sciences, Statistical Analysis System), and industry database programs such as DB2 and SQL.

All-in-One Suite. Although certain highly specialized functions, such as visualization, may require a researcher to go outside a data-mining application, tasks of data querying, data transformation, and tabulation (similar to business intelligence reporting) can all be done inside the application.

Automation. A data-mining model developed by the researcher can be converted into an application for real-time data scoring. This is why data mining is the tool of choice powering major commerce activities (banking, online sales, and airlines) while relegating statistical testing into single-task and academic research.

Conclusions

Data may contain information essential to the improvement of educational quality with the potential of customizing individual students' learning experiences. Obtaining data is a deliberate endeavor that is often time- and resource consuming. Therefore, data are precious assets to an institution. They are rich sources to be mined to their full potential. If not carefully and fully explored, this great asset is underutilized—a precious resource wasted. It is worthwhile to venture into new territories and take full advantage of the technology advancement to better understand data and better inform instruction, research, and programs and services to better serve the students. As an interdisciplinary data analysis tool, data mining provides great potentials and opportunities for efficient retrieval of information and knowledge discovery.

References

Friedman, J. F. "Data Mining and Statistics: What's the Connection?" 1997. http://www.salfordsystems.com/doc/dm-stat.pdf. Accessed July 3, 2006.

Guttman, L. "The Illogic of Statistical Inference for Cumulative Science." *Applied Stochastic Models and Data Analysis,* 1985, *1,* 3–10.

Hand, D., Mannila, H., and Smyth, P. *Principles of Data Mining.* Boston: MIT Press, 2001.

Kelley, D. *The Art of Reasoning.* (2nd ed.) New York: Norton, 1994.

Kuonen, D. "Data Mining and Statistics: What Is the Connection?" *Data Administration Newsletter (TDAN.com),* 2004. http://www.tdan.com/i030fe01.htm. Accessed July 3, 2006.

Luan, J. "Moving Beyond Hypothesis: Get an Edge in Institutional Research with Data Mining." SPSS/AIR Webinar Series, Dec. 2005. http://www.spss.com/airseries. Accessed July 3, 2006.

Luan, J. "Using Academic Behavior Index (AB-Index) to Develop a Learner Typology for Managing Enrollment and Course Offerings: A Data Mining Approach". *IR Applications,* July 2006. http://www.airweb.org/?page=566. Accessed July 3, 2006.

Mahoney, M. "Publication Prejudices: An Experimental Study of Confirmatory Bias in the Peer Review System." *Cognitive Therapy Research,* 1977, *1,* 161–175.

Mena, J. "Data Mining FAQs." *DM Review,* 1998. http://www.dmreview.com/master.cfm?NavID=198&EdID=792. Accessed July 3, 2006.

O'Connor, J. J., and Robertson, E. F. "John Wilder Tukey." 2006. http://wwwhistory.mcs.st-andrews.ac.uk/Biographies/Tukey.html. Accessed July 3, 2006.

Schield, M. "Statistical Literacy: Thinking Critically About Statistics." *Of Significance,* 1999, *1*(1). http://www.augsburg.edu/ppages/~schield/MiloPapers/984StatisticalLiteracy6.pdf. Accessed July 3, 2006.

Serban, A. M., and Luan, J. (eds.). *Knowledge Management: Building a Competitive Advantage in Higher Education.* New Directions for Institutional Research, no. 113. San Francisco: Jossey-Bass, 2002.

Tukey, J. W. "The Future of Data Analysis." *Annals of Mathematical Statistics,* 1962, *33,* 1–67.

Willett, T. *Assessing the Digital Divide: An Extension of the Pulse of the Community Survey.* Gilroy, Calif.: Galivan College Research Publication, 2004.

CHUN-MEI ZHAO *is research scholar, the Carnegie Foundation for the Advancement of Teaching.*

JING LUAN *is vice chancellor of Educational Services and Planning at San Mateo Community College District in California.*

2

Focusing on student retention and time to degree completion, this study illustrates how institutional researchers may benefit from the power of predictive analyses associated with data-mining tools.

Estimating Student Retention and Degree-Completion Time: Decision Trees and Neural Networks Vis-à-Vis Regression

Serge Herzog

Understanding student enrollment behavior is a central focus of institutional research in higher education. However, in the eyes of an enrollment management professional, the capacity to explain why students drop out, why they transfer out, or why some graduate quickly while others take their time may be less critical than the ability to accurately predict such events. Being able to identify who is at risk of dropping out or who is likely to take a long time to graduate helps target intervention programs to where they are needed most and offers ways to improve enrollment, graduation rate, and precision of tuition revenue forecasts.

Explanatory models by regression and path analysis have contributed substantially to our understanding of student retention (Adam and Gaither, 2005; Pascarella and Terenzini, 2005; Braxton, 2000), although the cumulative research on time to degree (TTD) completion is less impressive. A likely explanation for this is the more complex nature of the path to graduation, which has lengthened considerably over the past thirty years for a typical student (Knight, 2002, 2004; Noxel and Katunich, 1998; Council for Education Policy, Research and Improvement, 2002). Thus, whereas

The author thanks SPSS, Inc., for the demonstration version of their Clementine software used in this study.

prediction models for student retention have benefited greatly from more extensive analyses of factors associated with enrollment outcomes, factors influencing TTD completion are less understood. Therefore, developing models to estimate TTD completion is more difficult because research in this area has not matured to the same level.

Yet, comparing the prediction accuracies of these events (that is, retention and TTD completion) actually provides a useful framework to evaluate the relative potentials of different data analysis approaches. Namely, are there significant differences in prediction accuracy between data-mining tools and more traditional techniques when estimating outcomes of varying levels of complexity? Complexity in the data is typically associated with quality, quantity, and interaction of predictor variables and the number of possible outcomes in the dependent variable. To test for such differences, this study compares the prediction accuracy of three decision tree and three artificial neural network approaches with that of multinomial logistic regression. Findings are translated into operationally meaningful indicators in the context of enhanced institutional research on student retention, enrollment forecasting, and graduation rate analysis. Although the selection of predictor variables is guided by the research on retention and degree completion, the discussion focuses on which approach promises greatest prediction accuracy, not on how well either event is explained based on model fit and variable selection.

Prediction Accuracy of Data-Mining Techniques

Published studies on the use and prediction accuracy of data-mining approaches in institutional research are few. Luan (2002) illustrated the application of neural network and decision tree analysis in predicting the transfer of community college students to four-year institutions, concluding that a classification and regression tree (C&RT) algorithm yielded overall better accuracy than a neural network. Estimating the application behavior of potential freshmen who submitted admission test scores to a large research university, Byers González and DesJardins (2002) showed neural network accuracy to be superior over a binary logistic regression approach. A four-percentage point improvement in the overall correct classification rate with the neural network is extended by an additional two percentage points when continuous variables are used in lieu of dummy types. Maximizing accuracy in this way is possible with neural networks because they accommodate non-linearity and missing values among variables. Van Nelson and Neff (1990) conducted a similar comparative study of two neural networks and a linear regression function that yielded comparable results.

Failure to produce better results with the neural network solutions may be due to the small sample (fewer than five hundred) employed because neural networks typically work best with larger data sets. Using both cognitive and noncognitive variables to predict algebra proficiency—to improve course placement or admission selection—Everson, Chance, and Lykins (1994) contrasted three variations of neural networks with both a linear regression model and discriminant function analysis. Relying on a relatively small sample of six hundred cases, the study employed a cross-validation strategy based on ten training and test subsets of randomly selected cases to infer a population measure for all approaches. The neural networks outperformed the two traditional techniques, achieving higher average coefficients of determination (R^2) and number of correctly classi-fied cases. Although not focused on the issue of prediction accuracy per se, Thomas and Galambos (2004) demonstrated how decision tree analysis enriched the understanding of students' satisfaction with their college experience. Employing a chi-squared automatic interaction detector (CHAID) algorithm, they showed how displayed tree structures revealed patterns in the data that reflected heterogeneity among students that was elusive to regression analysis alone.

Examples outside the higher education domain further illuminate the potential utility of data-mining approaches. Concerned about the sustain-ability of runaway public school spending—with a 540 percent increase in constant-dollar-per-pupil expenditure from 1940 to 1990—Baker and Richards (1999) applied neural network solutions, using both standard and log-transformed data, to forecast future spending levels. Comparing the pre-diction accuracy of these models with one that replicated a multiple linear regression model used by the National Center for Education Statistics (NCES) for its annual projections, the study confirmed higher prediction accuracy with the neural networks. Surprisingly, those limited to linear pre-dictors attained the highest accuracy, about twice the level of the NCES regression model, a finding the authors suggested was due to the relatively high linearity of nationally aggregated annual data employed by the study. Using thirty-five different data sets ranging from one thousand to two mil-lion records, Perlich, Provost, and Simonoff (2003) contrasted logistic regression with decision tree analysis to predict a variety of binary outcomes (such as customer type at a bookstore, contraceptive methods for women, bank credit approval, presence of diabetes, online shopping behavior, and so on). They found that tree induction yielded better classification results on larger data sets than on smaller ones.

The influence of data size on prediction performance was also reflected in a study by Long, Griffith, Selker, and D'Agostino (1993), which arrived at comparable accuracy levels for both the decision tree and logistic regres-sion. The lack of superior performance with tree induction may have been due to the use of the older C4 algorithm. Estimating the level of aerobic fit-ness in adults, Tamminen, Laurinen, and Röning (1999) tested the accuracy of a C&RT versus neural networks and concluded that the latter provided better results. The advantage of using ensembles of resampled data for each prediction or classification in a decision tree (such as the C5.0), referred to as "bagging" and "boosting," was discussed in Opitz and Maclin (1999) and Roe and others (2005). Results from their studies showed that a boosting algorithm may improve prediction by 80 percent over the standard algorithm of a neural network, depending on the characteristics of the data set, the number of predictors, and the size of the tree structure. Boosting is a function of the greater weight attached to misclassified records in the course of sequentially built models from the resampled data, with the final prediction based on aggregate results from all the models.

This brief review of studies shows that data-mining methods offer distinct advantages over traditional statistics. Particularly when working with large data sets to estimate outcomes with many predictor variables, data-mining methods often yield greater prediction accuracy, classification accuracy, or both. However, higher education research provides little insight into which specific data-mining method to use when predicting key outcomes such as retention or degree completion.

Data Sources, Samples, and Variables

Based on students at a moderately selective Carnegie doctoral degree and research university, I accessed three sources to generate the data file: the institutional student information system for student demographic, academic, residential, and financial aid information; the American College Test (ACT)'s Student Profile Section for parent income data; and the National Student Clearinghouse for identifying transfer-out students. Retention predictions are based on the second-year enrollment of 8,018 new full-time freshmen who started in the fall semesters of 2000 through 2003 (or 96 percent of the total cohort, excluding varsity athletes, non-degree-seeking, and foreign students). Another data set used for the TTD-completion analysis captured end-of-fourth-year information of 15,457 undergraduate degree recipients from spring 1995 through summer 2005 (or 99 percent of all recipients after listwise deletion of incomplete records; the first degree received was counted for 85 multiple-degree holders). Forty predictors were used to estimate retention, and seventy-nine variables were included in the more complex TTD forecasts.

Variable selection for the retention predictions reflected an established institutional model to identify at-risk freshmen, as I described elsewhere (2005). Given the importance of first-year curricular experience in the established retention model, course experiences in core areas of the undergraduate experience guided the selection of many variables in the model development for TTD estimation. Variables are listed in Appendix A (at the end of this chapter) by cluster area and identified by type, with additional definitions furnished in Appendix B to ensure clarity of what is measured. Missing values for 493 cases were imputed for the variable measuring the ratio of earned-to-attempted credits by multiple regression ($R^2 = 0.70$); a general linear model was used to impute total campus-based credits for 804 cases ($R^2 = 0.68$). Mean value substitution was performed on 230 missing ACT scores.

NEW DIRECTIONS FOR INSTITUTIONAL RESEARCH • DOI: 10.1002/ir

Analytical Approach

The comparison of prediction accuracy is based on contrasting three-rule induction decision trees (C&RT, CHAID-based, and C5.0) and three back-propagation neural networks (simple topology, multitopology, and three-hidden-layer pruned) with a multinomial logistic regression model. Statistical Package for the Social Sciences, Inc.'s Clementine software version 9.0 was employed, and a brief description of each technique in Appendix C reflects algorithms used by the application and run methods and modeling options available. Detailed accounts of decision tree and neural network theory and application can be found in Murthy (1998), Berry and Linoff (2000), and Garson (1998).

Second-year retention was examined at the end of both the first and the second terms. For practical reasons and for the varying data complexity, the TTD analysis was conducted with and without transfer students to account for their typically distinct path to graduation. To validate prediction accuracy of each method used (that is, the statistical algorithm used), data sets were partitioned through a 50:50 randomized split to allow generated models based on training data to be tested on the holdout samples. The following retention outcomes are estimated: returned for second year (fall to fall), transferred out within one year, and dropped or stopped out for at least one year; degree completion time (TTD) outcomes are estimated for three years or less, four years, five years, and six years or more. This categorization generates a more balanced outcome in the dependent variable and ensures convergence in the regression model.

The profile of the cohort used for the retention analysis is summarized as follows: 56 percent were female students, 7 percent were Asian American, 3 percent were African American, 7 percent were Hispanic, and a little more than 1 percent were Native American. Fifty-six percent resided within commuting distance, and 11 percent were out-of-state residents. Twenty-six percent came from a low-income background, and 18 percent were high-income students. Thirteen percent entered with no financial aid, 19 percent took out student loans, 13 percent received Pell grants, and 68 percent used only forms of gift aid (scholarships and grants). Twenty percent took summer courses before their initial fall enrollment, and 14 percent entered with advanced placement credits. On average, students entered with an ACT score of 23.

Of the graduated students used for the TTD analysis, 57 percent were female, 8 percent were minority students (excluding Asian Americans), 70 percent resided within commuting distance of the campus, and 21 percent were out-of-state students. The average age at graduation was 27 years, and 20 percent were continuously enrolled (that is, never stopped out), 40 percent entered as transfer students (68 percent of whom came from in-state institutions), 16 percent started with an undeclared program major, and 19 percent graduated with honor (with any type of distinction).

NEW DIRECTIONS FOR INSTITUTIONAL RESEARCH • DOI: 10.1002/ir

Before training the models for a given outcome estimation, data miners typically explore the data to identify patterns among variables for guidance during the model-building process. For example, would merit-based student aid go to fast degree completers with strong academic records? As Figure 2.1 shows, more merit aid is indeed allocated to faster completers with higher grades. Less obvious is the impact of taking courses taught by adjunct faculty. As Figure 2.2 reveals, students finishing up within three years or less are more likely exposed to adjunct instructors. Because estimates of the TTD completion are based on a large number of predictors, whose interaction is not well understood, caution should be exercised in interpreting the contribution of a given variable in the model.

Prediction Accuracy of Tested Models

A comparison of the tested models' percentage of correctly predicted cases across all outcomes combined, based on the validation data sets, is depicted in Figure 2.3 for retention and Figures 2.4 and 2.5 for TTD completion. The overall prediction accuracy level with the validation data sets was within a few percentage points of the training sets, except for the C5.0 models, which

Figure 2.1. Merit Aid, Grades, and Degree Completion Time

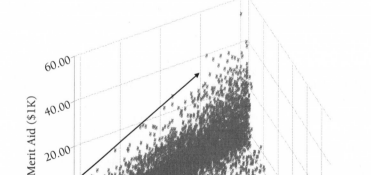

Figure 2.2. Exposure to Adjunct Faculty and Time to Degree (TTD)

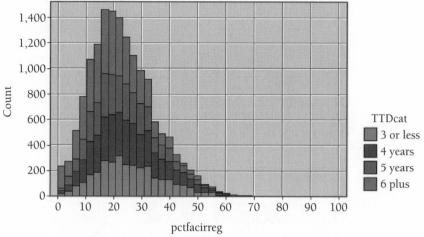

Note: The horizontal axis represents the percentage of teachers who are on nontenure track or have irregular contracts.

on average dropped by about fifteen percentage points. Although some of the tree and neural net algorithms yielded slightly higher levels of retention prediction over the baseline regression model, that advantage did not appear compelling with either the end-of-fall or end-of-spring data. Accuracy did

Figure 2.3. Model Comparison for Freshmen Retention: Overall Prediction Accuracy with Validation Data

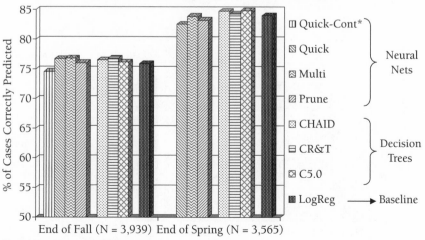

Note: *Continuous variables.

Figure 2.4. Model Comparison for Degree Completion Time: Prediction Accuracy with Validation Data, Three Years or Less

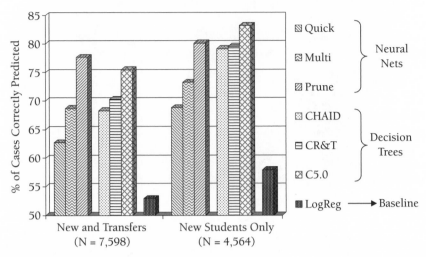

improve by almost ten percentage points as richer information became available at the end of the spring over the fall, but that improvement accrued with the baseline model also. The multitopology neural network performed significantly better in identifying dropout-stop-out students but poorly vis-à-vis the regression model in estimating who is likely to transfer out. The absence of more impressive results with the decision trees and neural net-

Figure 2.5. Model Comparison for Degree Completion Time: Prediction Accuracy with Validation Data, Six Years or More

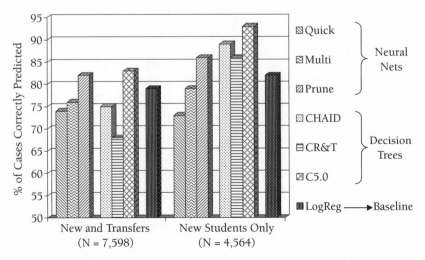

works was likely due to, among other things, the selection of variables exhibiting little collinearity and interaction effects during the development of the baseline regression model.

Overall prediction results in the TTD models, both with and without the inclusion of transfer students, showed substantial differences. When new and transfer students were examined together, the neural network with three hidden layers achieved a twenty-five-percentage point improvement in correctly predicted cases over the regression model, an overall accuracy of almost 50 percent greater. A similar improvement was achieved with the three decision trees and pruned neural network when the analysis was limited to new students. Further data reduction by excluding transfer students led to more improvement in accuracy for all models (see Figure 2.5). However, the "overall accuracy" discussed herein may not be as meaningful to the institution if its operational interest is focused on identifying those who are predicted to be taking longer to graduate. Hence, in this context, attention is placed on correctly identifying those expected to take six years or more, given that the six-year graduation rate has become a national benchmark for moderately selective institutions. The advantage of using any of the tested decision trees and the pruned neural network is even more pronounced when transfer students were excluded from the data set, with the best model, the C5.0, yielding an accuracy of 93 percent, or eleven percentage points higher than the baseline model. Thus, the potential advantage gained with any one model must be weighed in terms of which outcome is most effective in assisting the development of a successful student intervention program.

The decision trees and neural networks performed especially well in correctly predicting the relatively few students who graduated within three years or less when the data set was restricted to new students; conversely, the regression model performed comparably on the six-years-or-more outcome, given the level of prediction difficulty associated with that outcome. Hence, performance evaluation scores were almost identical for all tested models when predicting students who take six years or more but were notably lower for the regression model when estimating who graduated quickly. A confidence level report, available through the analysis node, further assisted the analyst in interpreting the prediction accuracy for *each* record in the data set. Mean confidence levels for all records confirmed better results for the decision trees and the regression model than for the neural networks, except in predicting TTD for all students, where the pruned neural network scored the highest. Comparing threshold scores for a specified level of accuracy—for example, the level achieved with the baseline approach—may further illuminate which technique is most preferred.

Output from the sensitivity analysis produced by the neural networks showed which predictors weighed in the most when estimating retention and degree completion time. In the latter case, neural networks identified credit hour–related predictors, student age, residency, and stop-out time among the most valuable. Similarly, credit hours, residency, and stop-out time had the largest beta coefficients in the regression model. However, unlike the baseline model, the neural networks also were able to use a student's program major, the trend in grades over time (defined in Appendix B), and exposure to adjunct faculty as effective correlates of TTD. In turn, the regression approach benefited more from knowing a student's English experience (including English 102 grade and English transfer credits) in the estimation process. A look at the hierarchy of generated rules in the decision trees showed that a student's age, average credit load, and grade-related predictors result in early splits in the induction process. These results confirm that enrollment intensity—as it relates to credit load per term, stop-out behavior, and dropped courses—is a key indicator in estimating graduation time. But as the neural network findings suggested, the first program major selected, the number of times a student changes his or her major, grades over time (the GPA trend), and even the type of faculty by whom the students are taught all contribute to a more accurate prediction.

Implications and Conclusions

Having examined the prediction accuracy of several data-mining methods, all relatively new to institutional research, and compared it with that of logistic regression, a well-established approach, the study found that the level of complexity of the data used and the outcome predicted may largely guide the selection of a particular analytical tool. Predicting freshmen retention based on inferential statistics with little collinearity among variables may not be the best use of decision tree or neural net methods. On average, the decision trees and neural networks performed at least as good as the regression model, but the number and type of variables used as predictors—and repeatedly tested and adjusted in previous regression models—did not confer a substantial advantage to the data-mining methods.

However, the data-mining algorithms worked notably better with the larger set of exploratory predictors used to estimate the degree completion time, an outcome not as well studied as student retention. In the most complex analysis, where time to graduation is estimated for new and transfer students simultaneously, the pruned neural network with three hidden layers and the C5.0 decision tree performed best. The different results from the three neural networks confirm the importance of exploring available setup options in the application's neural network node. For example, adding multiple hidden layers and removing underused neurons (pruning) greatly raised the accuracy level compared with the less impressive results with the simple-topology model. Similarly, applying an error-weighted boosting factor to misclassifications in the C5.0 model may yield further improvements, as demonstrated in other studies discussed in the literature review section.

Decision tree and neural network approaches may expand the analyst's understanding of what variables contribute to prediction accuracy when working with large data sets. Sensitivity analysis helped identify important

NEW DIRECTIONS FOR INSTITUTIONAL RESEARCH • DOI: 10.1002/ir

predictors beyond those highlighted in the regression model. Intuitively, one may expect credit load and stop-out time to be related to degree completion time. But what about the type of teaching faculty? That variable, and other less obvious ones, attained fairly high sensitivity scores in the neural network results; in contrast, the baseline regression model showed little statistical significance associated with the type of faculty. Thus, getting the most out of working with large sets of predictor variables is easier with data-mining tools that rank predictors on a single metric. Sensitivity scores from this study are instrumental in guiding the development of simplified models and may eliminate variables over which the institution has little control. For example, among the many financial aid measures used in the TTD analysis, only three scored relatively high on the sensitivity scale, namely, whether a student received a state-funded merit scholarship, the total amount of loans received, and the total amount of aid received from any source. Identifying all sources of aid separately does not appear to contribute much to prediction accuracy. Similarly, knowing whether a student took a remedial math course added little in the presence of indicators measuring math performance (grades) across all introductory math classes.

The operational impact of this study on the institution centers on how many additional students who are "at risk" could be correctly identified in due course to allow for effective intervention. Because data-mining techniques scarcely differed from the regression model in overall prediction accuracy and produced inconsistent results in estimating dropout or stop-out versus transfer-out risk in the retention analysis—except, of course, that data-mining application allows automation in scoring future data, which cannot be matched by conventional statistical tools. Compared with the baseline approach, improved prediction accuracy with the multilayer pruned neural network and the C5.0 would yield an additional 105 to 140 correctly identified students at risk of taking at least six years or more to graduate (or 3 to 4 percent of approximately 3,500 undergraduates enrolled after four years). If the prediction is restricted to only students who started as new freshmen, the advantage would range from 170 to 270 (or 7 to 11 percent of approximately 2,450 students).

Because the institution is likely to experience continued strong enrollment growth over the next ten years, the number of additional students who can be identified as at risk will grow commensurately. The benefit of correctly targeting hundreds of additional students each year with appropriate counseling and academic support is difficult to gauge because potential benefits are a function of the effectiveness of the program(s) put in place to promote faster degree completion. But an intervention can proceed with more confidence on knowing that resources are allocated to the right students.

Improvement in the degree completion time by better identification of at-risk students translates not only to higher graduation rates but also to substantial cost savings for students. By way of illustration, timely counseling prompted by a newly identified at-risk student may well obviate the occurrence of a change in program major, which is associated with lengthening time to graduation. Barrow and Rouse (2005) put the total cost of a four-year degree at over $107,000 for the average student who entered college in 2003 and who will graduate in four years. About 72 percent of that total cost is due to the opportunity cost of lost wages (which equal average annual earnings of a high school graduate). Adding the difference in lifetime earnings over forty years between a college graduate and a high school graduate, and assuming an average six-year degree completion time, which approximates conditions at the institution, speeding up time to graduation by one year may save a student around $28,000 in forgone earnings (not counting a likely higher increment of tuition and fees for a six-year graduate compared with a five-year graduate). Faster completion reduces both the net attendance cost and the time to recoup the educational investment cost once gainfully employed. Finally, better estimates of how long students take to graduate may help improve enrollment projections that are used for institutional planning purposes (for example, construction of new classroom buildings).

Current projections are in part based on how quickly students move from one class standing to the next (such as from freshman to sophomore), as expressed in the conversion ratio (that is, the percentage of sophomores in year 2 who were freshmen in year 1). Projected numbers are also disaggregated by demographic attributes, such as student age, gender, or ethnicity. Running data mining–based estimates of degree completion time with data similarly disaggregated may help improve enrollment projections through adjusted conversion ratios in the model. For example, a drop from one year to the next in the estimated proportion of students taking six years or more to graduate may well suggest a need to lower the conversion ratio to project the number of returning seniors in the future (that is, a greater proportion of seniors in the previous year will graduate). Being able to more accurately predict how many students graduate within a given time frame through demographic and academic attributes will help refine future enrollment projections. Such projections may also benefit from information associated with variables that are useful to data mining–based estimates but cannot be used under the more restrictive statistical assumptions that govern regression analyses.

References

Adam, J., and Gaither, G. H. "Retention in Higher Education: A Selective Resource Guide." In G. H. Gaither (ed.), *Minority Retention: What Works?* New Directions for Institutional Research, no. 125. San Francisco: Jossey-Bass, 2005.

Baker, B., and Richards, C. "A Comparison of Conventional Linear Regression Methods and Neural Networks for Forecasting Educational Spending." *Economics of Education Review,* 1999, *18,* 405–415.

Barrow, L., and Rouse, C. "Does College Still Pay?" *Economists' Voice,* 2005, 2(4), 1–8.

Berry, M., and Linoff, G. *Master Data Mining: The Art and Science of Customer Relationship Management.* New York: Wiley Computer, 2000.

Braxton, J. *Reworking the Student Departure Puzzle.* Nashville, Tenn.: Vanderbilt University Press, 2000.

Byers González, J., and DesJardins, S. "Artificial Neural Networks: A New Approach for Predicting Application Behavior." *Research in Higher Education,* 2002, *43*(2), 235–258.

Council for Education Policy, Research and Improvement [CEPRI]. "Postsecondary Progression of 1993–94 Florida Public High School Graduates: 2002 Update." *To the Point,* August 2002. http://www.cepri.state.fl.us. Accessed Nov. 18, 2005.

Everson, H., Chance, D., and Lykins, S. "Using Artificial Neural Networks in Educational Research: Some Comparisons with Linear Statistical Models." Paper presented at the American Educational Research Association Conference, New Orleans, April 5–7, 1994. (ED 372 094)

Garson, G. *Neural Networks: An Introductory Guide for Social Scientists.* London: Sage, 1998.

Herzog, S. "Measuring Determinants of Student Return vs. Dropout/Stopout vs. Transfer: A First-to-Second Year Analysis of New Freshmen." *Research in Higher Education,* 2005, *46*(8), 883–928.

Knight, W. "Toward a Comprehensive Model of Influences upon Time to Bachelor's Degree Attainment." *AIR Professional File,* 2002, *85*(Winter).

Knight, W. "Time to Bachelor's Degree Attainment: An Application of Descriptive, Bivariate, and Multiple Regression Techniques." *IR Applications,* 2, Sept. 8, 2004. http://airweb.org/page/asp?page=628. Accessed Oct. 15, 2004.

Long, W., Griffith, J., Selker, H., and D'Agostino, R. "A Comparison of Logistic Regression to Decision-Tree Induction in a Medical Domain." *Computers in Biomedical Research,* 1993, *26,* 74–97.

Luan, J. "Data Mining and Its Applications in Higher Education." In A. M. Serban and J. Luan (eds.), *Knowledge Management: Building a Competitive Advantage in Higher Education.* New Directions for Institutional Research, no. 113. San Francisco: Jossey-Bass, 2002.

Murthy, S. "Automatic Construction of Decision Trees from Data: A Multi-Disciplinary Survey." *Data Mining and Knowledge Discovery,* 1998, 2, 345–389.

Noxel, S., and Katunich, L. "Navigating for Four Years to the Baccalaureate Degree." Paper presented at the Association for Institutional Research Conference, Minneapolis, May 17–20, 1998. (ED 422 825)

Opitz, D., and Maclin, R. "Popular Ensemble Methods: An Empirical Study." *Journal of Artificial Intelligence Research,* 1999, *11,* 169–198.

Pascarella, E., and Terenzini, P. *How College Affects Students.* San Francisco: Jossey-Bass, 2005.

Perlich, C., Provost, F., and Simonoff, J. "Tree Induction vs. Logistic Regression: A Learning-Curve Analysis." *Journal of Machine Learning Research,* 2003, *4,* 211–255.

Roe, B., and others. "Boosted Decision Trees as an Alternative to Artificial Neural Networks for Particle Identification." *Nuclear Instruments and Methods in Physics Research,* 2005, *543,* 577–584.

Tamminen, S., Laurinen, P., and Röning, J. "Comparing Regression Trees with Neural Networks in Aerobic Fitness Approximation." Proceedings of the International Computing Sciences Conference Symposium on Advances in Intelligent Data Analysis, Rochester, N.Y., June 22–25, 1999, pp. 414–419.

Thomas, E., and Galambos, N. "What Satisfies Students? Mining Student-Opinion Data with Regression and Decision Tree Analysis." *Research in Higher Education,* 2004, *45*(3), 251–269.

Van Nelson, C., and Neff, K. "Comparing and Contrasting Neural Network Solutions to Classical Statistical Solutions." Paper presented at the Midwestern Educational Research Association Conference, Chicago, Oct. 19, 1990. (ED 326 577).

SERGE HERZOG is director of institutional analysis at the University of Nevada, Reno.

NEW DIRECTIONS FOR INSTITUTIONAL RESEARCH • DOI: 10.1002/ir

Appendix A: Predictors

Retention Analysis

Student Demographics
Gender[a]
Age[b,c]
Ethnicity or race[d]
Residency[d]
Parent income[d]

Precollegiate Experience
High school grade-point average (GPA)[b]
American College Test (ACT) English or math scores[b] (Scholastic Assessment Test [SAT] conversion)
ACT or SAT test date[b,c]
Academic preparation index[b,c]
Prefall summer enrollment[a]
Advanced placement or international baccalaureate (IB) credits[a]
Graduate degree aspiration[a]

Campus Experience
On-campus living[a]
Use of athletic facilities[a]
Dual enrollment with community college (CC)[a]
Fall entry term[d]
Attempted registrations[c]
Average class size[c]

Academic Experience
Academic peer challenge[c]
Fall or first-year GPA[b,c]
Credit load (<15 units)[a]
Major requires calculus 1[a]
Natural or physical science courses[c]
Remedial math taken[a]
Remedial English taken[a]
Math credits earned[c]

All and math transfer credits[a]
Fall or spring math grades[d]
Math D or F grades[a]
Math I or W grades[a]
Passed first-year math[a]
English 101 or 102 grades[d]
Program major type[d]

Financial Aid Need[b]
Fall and spring remaining
First-year total remaining
Fall and spring total need before total aid offered
Fall or spring package by type of aid included[d]
    No aid
    Package with loans, work study, or both
    Grants, scholarships only, or both
    Millennium scholarship only
Second-year package offer by type of aid included as above[d]
Fall or Spring Institutional Aid Amount ($)[b]
Second-Year Institutional Aid Amount Offered ($)[b]
Fall or Spring Pell Grant Aid[a]
Millennium Aid, Fall or Spring[d]
    Never had it
    Received it, maintains eligibility
    Lost eligibility, continues ineligibility
    Lost eligibility, regains eligibility

Time-to-Degree Analysis
Financial Aid
Total aid received[b]
Loans[b]
Grants[b]
Work study[b]
Merit-based aid[b]
Need-based aid[b]
General fund aid[b]

[a]Range or scale.
[b]Flag or binomial.
[c]Ordinal or rank.
[d]Set or multinomial.

NEW DIRECTIONS FOR INSTITUTIONAL RESEARCH • DOI: 10.1002/ir

Outside aid[b]
University of Nevada, Reno (UNR)
  Foundation aid[b]
Academic department-based aid[b]
Grants-in-aid[b]
Millennium Scholarship[b]
Pell Grant aid[b]

Student Demographics
Gender[a]
Age[b]
Ethnicity or race[d]
Residency[d]

Precollegiate Experience
ACT English[b]
ACT math[b]
ACT composite[b]

General Experience
Initial status (new versus transfer)[a]
Initial program major[d]
Program major in fourth year[d]
Number of program major changes[b]
Declared a minor[a]
Completed a senior thesis[a]
Attempted registrations[b]
Participated in varsity sports[a]
Stop-out time since first enrollment
  (percent)[b,c]

Course Grades
Remedial math[d]
College algebra[d]
College general math[d]
College trigonometry[d]
Introduction to statistics[d]
Business calculus[d]
Calculus 1[d]
English 101[d]
English 102[d]
Core humanities 201–203[d]
General capstone[d]
Program major capstone[d]
Cumulative GPA[b,c]

GPA trend[b]
Number of D or F grades (percent)[b]
Number of I or W grades (percent)[b]
Number of replacement grades[b]

Outside Course Experiences
Took overseas courses (USAC)[a]
Took continuing education courses[a]
Took courses at TMCC (local CC)[b]
Took courses at WNCC (local CC)[b]
Took internships[c]
English courses transferred in[c]
Math courses transferred in[c]
English distance courses[a]
Math distance courses[a]
Core humanities transferred in[c]

Campus Course Experiences
Took honors courses[a]
Took independent studies[c]
Repeated a course[a]
Took remedial math or English[a]
Capstone courses taken[b]
"Diversity" courses taken[b]
Natural science courses in three
  core areas (three variables)[b]

Credit Hours
Total credits accumulated[b]
Total transfer credits[b]
Total campus credits[b]
Total math credits[b]
Total upper-division science credits[b]
Total credits transferred in[b]
Earned:attempted credits (percent)[b]
Average credit load per enrolled
  term[b]

Faculty Teaching Courses Taken
Percentage of women[b]
Percentage of ethnic or racial
  minority[b]
Percentage of part-time faculty[b]
Percentage of adjunct faculty[b]
Percentage at full-professor rank[b]
Average age of faculty[b]

Appendix B: Variable Definitions

Initial study major Declared or premajor, undeclared, nondegree seeking, intensive English.

Attempted registrations Registration attempt at time of fully subscribed class section during registration period.

Stop-out time Number of fall or spring semesters not in attendance after first campus-based course enrollment.

Number of replacement grades Students may repeat up to twelve lower-division credits to replace original grades at institution.

Grade-point average (GPA) trend Ratio of twenty-four-credit GPA to cumulative GPA after fourth year.

Natural sciences core course offerings geared for three groups of majors Social science, natural science, and engineering.

Parent income Grouped into upper, middle, and bottom thirds with a "missing" category for students without a federal aid application and without data from the American College Test (ACT) Student Profile Section.

ACT English and math scores A Scholastic Assessment Test (SAT)-ACT conversion table was used for students with only SAT scores.

Appendix C: Model Descriptions and Generated Characteristics for Time-to-Degree (TTD) Models

CHAID Chi-squared automatic interaction detector; uses chi-squared statistics to identify optimal splits with two or more subgroups. Starts with most significant predictor, determines multiple-group differences, and collapses groups with no significance; the merging process stops at the preset testing level. Generated tree depth: 4.

C&RT Classification and regression tree; generates splits based on maximizing orthogonality between subgroups (measured by the Gini index of diversity); all splits are binary, and outcome variable can be continuous or categorical. Generated tree depth: 5.

C5.0 Uses the 5.0 algorithm to generate a decision tree or rule set based on the predictor that provides maximum information gain. The split process continues until the sample is exhausted. Lowest-level splits are removed if they fail to contribute to model significance. Generated tree depth: 4, no boosting; rules for each outcome: 38, 23, 40, 53 (default outcome: four years).

Neural net simple topology (quick method) Using the software default settings for learning rates (alpha and eta decay), this is a one-hidden-layer model with 158 nodes at the input, 8 in the hidden layer, and 4 at the output.

Neural net multiple topologies Creates several networks in parallel based on a specified number of hidden layers and nodes in each layer. Used default learning rates, with 158 input nodes, 5 nodes in the hidden layer and 4 at the output for the final solution; initial parallel networks with 2 to 20 nodes in one hidden layer and 2 to 27 and 2 to 22 nodes in two hidden layers, respectively.

Neural net prune method Starts with a large network of layers and nodes as specified and removes (prunes) weakest nodes in input and hidden layers during training. Three hidden layers were specified, with the following number of nodes from input to output: 38, 4, 2, 2, and 4.

Logistic regression Direct variable entry with main effects output only, resulting in a pseudo R^2 of 0.728 (Cox and Snell); likelihood convergence set on default.

3

This case study represents an initial attempt by a university to employ data-mining techniques to study a ternary attrition variable produced by integrating multiple internal and external databases.

Considering Student Mobility in Retention Outcomes

Sutee Sujitparapitaya

High student attrition rates are of immediate concern to all. Studies have shown that the most vulnerable stage for student retention at all institutions of higher education, including highly selective colleges and universities, is the first year of college (Learning Slope, 1991). More than half of the students who withdraw from college do so during their first year (Consortium for Student Retention Data Exchange, 2000), resulting in a first-year attrition rate of more than 25 percent at four-year institutions (American College Test [ACT], 2001). Because the seeds of leaving university tend to be planted early, it is important for institutions to identify these students early in their academic careers and tailor institutional support and intervention programs to the improvement in retention outcomes.

About one in five students who earn a bachelor's degree receives it from a four-year college other than the one in which he or she originally enrolled (Adelman, 2004). It is evident that data from a single institution would not be sufficient to explain student transfer-out behavior. Several sources of data from multiple time frames are necessary to track students' movement after leaving an institution. As a central agency for college lenders of financial aid, the National Student Clearinghouse (NSC) has developed and currently maintains a national database that tracks students across more than 90 percent of institutions of higher learning in the United States (National Student Clearinghouse, 2004). The NSC data, in combination with institutional databases and the advancement of quantitative data-mining tools, allow

NEW DIRECTIONS FOR INSTITUTIONAL RESEARCH, no. 131, Fall 2006   © Wiley Periodicals, Inc.
Published online in Wiley InterScience (www.interscience.wiley.com) • DOI: 10.1002/ir.186

institutions to use learned information to predict the likelihood of both stop-out and transfer-out behaviors.

This case study was done to examine critical predictors influencing the decisions of first-time freshmen on completion of their first year (one-year retention). The outcome variable, freshmen's decision, has three options: remaining at their current institution, transferring to other postsecondary institutions, or stopping out from returning to higher education during the period of study. Therefore, it is a ternary variable. The study combined NSC's tracking data and the institution's internal databases and compared and contrasted three data-mining predictive modeling techniques—multinomial logistic regression, C5.0 rule induction, and neural network—to arrive at the final set of predictors. Influential factors include three primary categories: preparation for university study, including precollege experience and remediation; academic outcomes and enrollment behaviors; and student background.

The study described in this chapter showcases how data mining has been applied in student retention work. The chapter contains four primary sections. In the first section is described data collection procedures and integration of the NSC data with institutional databases. In the second, the research design that elicits influential variables is discussed, and the statistical treatments (listed above), using a comprehensive data-mining tool developed by SPSS, Inc., and called Clementine, are presented. In the third section, I describe the first-year retention model using the three-outcome variable and discuss the results. In the final section is a summary and discussion of the study's potential impact with regard to promoting graduation and retention.

Data Collection

In most retention studies, students' decisions to return after the end of their first year have been described as either retained or dropped out. Because of a lack of relevant information on students who were not retained, stop-outs have been inappropriately combined with transfer-outs. Because the NSC database tracks enrolled students across institutions, the institutions were able to integrate the NSC data with their internal data to expand the retention model to account for students who either transferred out to other postsecondary institutions or stopped out from postsecondary education before the beginning of their second year.

With the NSC data, institutions are able to obtain a more complete picture of their first-year student persistence. Table 3.1 shows one-year persistence of the fall 2003 first-time freshmen. The data in Column A suggest that 20.5% percent of the entire first-time freshmen did not return to the same institution after one year. Of those, 12.8 percent did not drop out but instead transferred to another institution. The focus of Column B was on only nonreturning students (both stop-outs and transfer-outs). As shown, 62.8 percent of those who did not return actually transferred to another institution. Among those institutions, California community colleges

Table 3.1. One-Year Persistence of the Fall 2003 First-Time Freshmen Cohort

	Head Count	A Cohort (%)	B Transferred Out and Stopped Out (%)
Entire FTF cohort	2,444	100.0	
Retained	1,944	79.5	
Not retained	500	20.5	100.0
Stopped out	186	7.6	37.2
Transferred out	314	12.8	62.8
Calif. 4-year (CSU)	13	0.5	2.6
Calif. 4-year (UC)	1	0.0	0.2
Calif. 2-year (CCC)	284	11.6	56.8
Calif. 4-year (others)	3	0.1	0.6
Calif. 2-year (others)	1	0	0.2
Out-of-state 4-year	9	0.4	1.8
Out-of-state 2-year	3	0.1	0.6

Note: CSU = California State University [system]; UC = University of California [system]; CCC = California community college; FTF = first-time freshmen.

Source: National Student Clearinghouse and institutional data.

accounted for 56.8 percent. This group that transfers from a four-year to a two-year institution before earning baccalaureate degrees has been referred to as *undergraduate reverse transfers.*

Data-Mining Design and Method

Factors that influence the enrollment outcomes in this study were based on three categories of student registration behaviors after their first year of college:

1. Reenrollment at their current institution at the beginning of the second year: retained;
2. Transfer to other postsecondary institutions (either two- or four-year universities): transferred out;
3. Discontinuing their postsecondary education altogether: stopped out.

The entire population of fall 2003 first-time freshmen at a large urban university were selected for this analysis. Table 3.2 presents descriptions of the fourteen influential factors, comprising three primary categories, that were used in this study and how they were scored.

Descriptive statistics of the influential factors in Table 3.3 suggest that students who were retained after one year tended to have better academic preparation before entering the university, as measured by high school GPA

Table 3.2. Factors That Influence Retention

Variable	Description
Preparation for university study	
High school GPA	Grade-point average
Remedial English: English Proficiency Test (EPT)	Coded 1 if student failed EPT, 0 otherwise (passed, exempted)
Remedial Math: Entry Level Math (ELM) exam	Coded 1 if student failed ELM, 0 otherwise (passed, exempted)
Application time	Number of days between the first day of classes and the admission application date
Admission basis	Coded 1 if student met all the regular admission criteria, 0 otherwise (exceptional, others)
Academic outcomes and enrollment behaviors	
College GPA	Cumulated college GPA at the end of first year
Undeclared major	Coded 1 if student had undeclared major during first semester, 0 otherwise
Units attempted during first semester	Total attempted units at the beginning of first semester
Student demographics	
Age	Age at time of matriculation (in years)
Gender	Coded 1 if female, 0 otherwise
California residency	Coded 1 if California state resident based on tuition status, 0 otherwise
Minority status	Coded 1 if student is a member of a minority group or international, 0 otherwise
Distance from home	Distance (in miles) between university and student's permanent address
Low-income family	Status based on poverty thresholds using size of family and annual family contribution

(3.238) and admission type (91 percent). In addition, they seemed to be more certain about pursuing a bachelor's degree as measured by more days. Most of the retained students submitted their admission application sooner and registered for higher units at the beginning of their first semester than those who decided to leave. As a matter of fact, this group had the highest level of performances compared with the stop-outs and the transfer-outs. During the academic year, students who were retained seemed to demonstrate better academic performance as measured by college GPA (2.699— again, the highest of all) after the end of the first year.

As shown in Table 3.3, the students who were retained tended to be from a minority group and female. Further, more of the students who stopped out or transferred were from low-income families.

NEW DIRECTIONS FOR INSTITUTIONAL RESEARCH • DOI: 10.1002/ir

Table 3.3. Descriptive Statistics of Influential Factors

Influential Factors	Stopped Out	Retained	Transferred Out
Preparation for university study			
High school GPA	3.2	3.2	3.1
Failed EPT (%)	41.9	42.8	37.3
Failed ELM (%)	52.7	51.3	49.0
Application time (days)	253	265	256
Regular admission (%)	88	91	86
Academic outcomes, enrollment behaviors, and financial aid			
College GPA	1.5	2.7	1.7
Good standing (%)	35	78	42
Undeclared major (%)	23	26	26
Total attempted units	13.5	14.5	13.76
Demographics			
Age (years)	18.3	18.2	18.2
Female (%)	53	61	57
California resident (%)	95	98	98
Minority (%)	59	60	55
Low-income family (%)	87	73	79

Data in an SPSS format of the fall 2003 first-time freshmen were directly read into Clementine and then divided into two equal data sets using the 50 percent random-split method: a training data set for the purpose of building the initial models and a separate test data set used to validate the model. The data from the training data set underwent analysis using three different algorithms: multinomial logistic regression, neural network, and C5.0. Neural network is based on machine learning and artificial intelligence. It contains an extra layer, called the hidden layer, which allows a far more mathematically complex computation to take place than a typical regression-based algorithm. C5.0 is a rule-based algorithm that produces sets of rules and decision tree graphics. Once the model(s) has learned the patterns inside the training data set and is able to make adequate predictions, data mining subjects the models to a new data set: the validation set. This represents a key difference between traditional statistical analysis and the data-mining approach to data analysis.

Suppose three models—A, C, and F—predicted with 85 percent accuracy the students who would be retained. Each of the three models should then be able to reach similar levels of accuracy on a fresh data set, which means in essence that the models have tested real-life data. The advantages of conducting model performance testing on a test data set over other approaches are clear. The traditional statistical analysis would rely primarily on *p* values and a host of other summary parameters to determine model performance. But this would provide only an overall model performance check, not necessarily an individual case-based performance check. This approach would not lead to conclusions on how the model would perform with real-life data.

Model Analysis

Three predictive modeling techniques used in predicting students' persistence behaviors were considered for model comparison: multinomial logistic regression, classification and decision tree (rule-induction-based algorithm), and neural networks. Because this study required access to a large database and the use of versatile and automated analysis, Clementine was chosen. It has powerful graphical user-interface features and a large number of analytical algorithms at its disposal, including traditional statistical algorithms (Figure 3.1).

Figure 3.1 displays the Clementine data streams that provide an interactive and iterative data-mining process to access data sources, transform data, determine variable features, uncover variable relationships, develop models, and generate outputs. Once the models had learned the patterns inside the training data set and were able to make predictions, the study

Figure 3.1. Data Streams for Both Training and Validating Data Flows

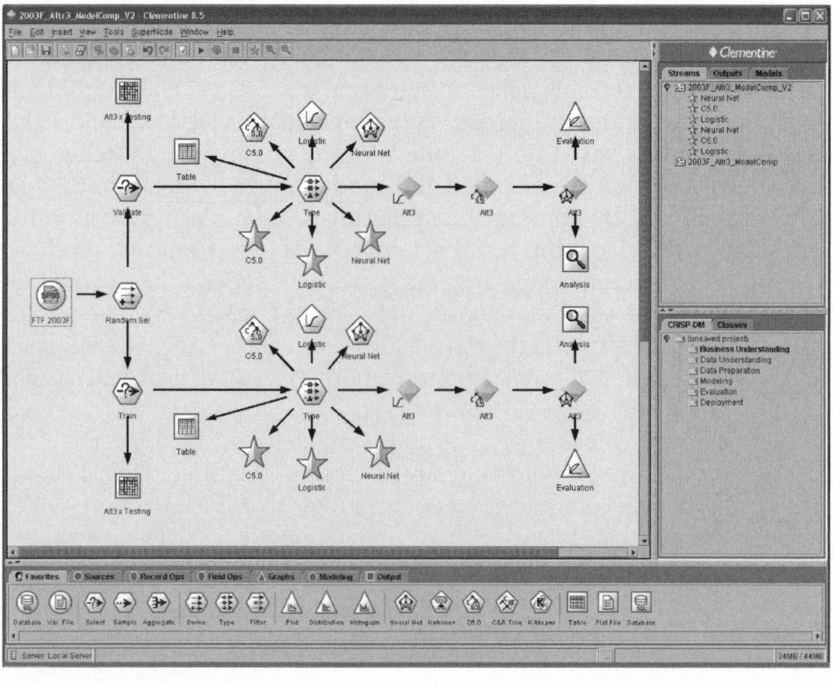

subjected the models to the test data set that they had not seen. To do so, the study used the known outcome variables to compare with the predicted outcomes. At the end of each stream, the analysis node and evaluation chart were used as a way of assessing the performance of predicted outcomes as well as comparing the performance across the models.

For the purpose of focusing more on the results of the study than the process, the different implementations of these techniques will not be described. Readers can refer to the chapters in Jing Luan's data mining textbook published in 2002.

Multinomial Logistic Regression. Multinomial logistic regression is selected when a dependent variable is discrete (two or more categories) rather than continuous. This technique calculates the probability of a particular record being a member of the target group, based on the values of the influential variables (Kleinbaum, 1994). The model used in this study attempts to predict three categories of student registration behavior after their first year at the same institution based on the information of preparation for university study, academic outcomes, enrollment behaviors, and general student background.

An overall model fit and a "final" model chi-square statistic were obtained to provide an omnibus test of effects in the model, with the following result: intercept only = 1,021.41 −2 log likelihood; final model = 777.53 −2 log likelihood χ^2, 243.88; *df*, 28; significance, .00. The chi-square statistic is the difference in −2 log likelihoods between the final model and a reduced model. The reduced model is formed by omitting an effect from the final model. The null hypothesis is that all parameters of that effect are zero. The 28 degrees of freedom correspond to the fourteen continuous influential variables in the model based on the change in −2 log likelihood. This change takes place from the initial model to the final iteration that suggests at least some effect in the model is significant.

Table 3.4 shows the results for predicting probability ratios of two separate sets of outcome: stopped out and transferred out. The intercept and the fourteen influential variables are listed with their beta coefficients, standard errors, a test of significance based on the Wald statistic, and the exponentiated value of the beta coefficient, along with its 95 percent confidence interval. Similar to ordinary linear regression, these coefficients are interpreted as estimates for the effect of a particular influential variable, controlling for the other thirteen variables in the equation. Cumulative college GPA and attempted units enrolled during the first semester have negative effects on both sets of retention outcome. In other words, an increase in these variables reduces the expected probability of being either a stop-out or transfer-out. The other variables with negative effects are the application time—the number of days between the first day of classes and the admission application date—for transfer-outs and in-state residency and high school GPA for stop-outs. A decrease in any of these variables is expected to correspond to an increase in the probability of being either a stop-out or a transfer-out. The amount of decrease expected would differ for each variable on the basis

Table 3.4. Parameter Estimates of College Retention Rates Using Multinomial Logistic Regression

Cohort	Factors	B	SE	Wald	df	Significance	Exponentiated B (95% Confidence Interval)		
1STOP	Intercept	4.624	6.087	0.577	1	.447			
	@1YrGPA	-0.022	0.002	87.618	1	.000	0.978	(0.974	-0.983)
	@1tmAUnt	-0.188	0.081	5.402	1	.020	0.828	(0.707	-0.971)
	AdmbCD	-1.062	0.550	3.733	1	.053	0.346	(0.118	-1.015)
	Age	0.037	0.309	0.014	1	.904	1.038	(0.567	-1.900)
	AppTm	-0.002	0.003	0.365	1	.546	0.998	(0.991	-1.005)
	Dist	-0.004	0.003	2.101	1	.147	0.996	(0.991	-1.001)
	ELMCD	-0.211	0.370	0.326	1	.568	0.810	(0.392	-1.672)
	EPTCD	0.094	0.369	0.065	1	.799	1.098	(0.533	-2.262)
	GenCD	0.249	0.353	0.498	1	.480	1.283	(0.642	-2.564)
	HSGPA	-0.706	0.357	3.907	1	.048	0.494	(0.245	-0.994)
	LInCD	0.044	0.467	0.009	1	.925	1.045	(0.419	-2.609)
	MinCD	1.373	0.483	8.065	1	.005	3.945	(1.530	-10.174)
	ResCD	-2.875	0.861	11.145	1	.001	5.643E-02	(1.044E-02	-0.305)
	UNDCD	-0.344	0.403	0.730	1	.393	0.709	(0.322	-1.561)

2TRNF	B	S.E.	Wald	df	Sig.	Exp(B)		
Intercept	17.193	5.652	9.253	1	.002			
@1YrGPA	-0.013	0.002	55.949	1	.000	0.987	0.984	(-0.990)
@1tmAUnt	-0.240	0.063	14.279	1	.000	0.787	0.695	(-0.891)
AdmbCD	-0.287	0.434	0.437	1	.508	0.750	0.320	(-1.757)
Age	-0.554	0.289	3.675	1	.055	0.575	0.326	(-1.012)
AppTm	-0.007	0.002	8.759	1	.003	0.993	0.989	(-0.998)
Dist	0.000	0.001	0.013	1	.910	1.000	0.998	(-1.003)
ELMCD	-0.089	0.276	0.105	1	.746	0.915	0.533	(-1.570)
EPTCD	-0.281	0.273	1.056	1	.304	0.755	0.442	(-1.290)
GenCD	-0.313	0.261	1.434	1	.231	0.731	0.438	(-1.220)
HSGPA	0.361	0.364	0.981	1	.322	1.434	0.703	(-2.928)
LInCD	-0.305	0.402	0.577	1	.447	0.737	0.335	(-1.620)
MinCD	-0.495	0.259	3.650	1	.056	0.610	0.367	(-1.013)
ResCD	-1.253	0.877	2.043	1	.153	0.286	5.121E-02	(-1.592)
UNDCD	0.067	0.272	0.060	1	.807	1.069	0.627	(-1.821)

Note: 1STOP = stop-outs; 2TRNF = transfer-outs; @1YrGPA = cumulated college grade-point average at the end of the first year; @1tmAUnt = cumulative earned units at the end of the first semester; AdmbCD = admission basis; Age = age (in years) at time of matriculation; AppTm = number of days between first day of classes and the admission application date; Dist = distance (in miles) between university and student's permanent address; ELMCD = remedial math: entry-level math exam (Coded 1 if passed or exempted, 0 if failed. Students who failed must enroll in remedial coursework as determined by their score.); EPTCD = remedial English: English proficiency test (Coded 1 if passed or exempted, 0 if failed. Students who failed must enroll in remedial coursework as determined by their score.); GenCD = gender: coded 1 if female, 0 otherwise; HSGPA = high school GPA; LInCD = low-income family; MinCD = minority status; ResCD = California residency; UNDCD = undeclared major.

of regression coefficients. Minority status is the only predictor with a positive effect on being a stop-out. This suggests that minority students have a higher chance than nonminority students of stopping out.

Table 3.5 provides a measure of how well the model performs. The rows of the table represent the actual outcome categories, and the columns are the predicted outcome categories. The overall predictive accuracy of the model is 84.3 percent. For individual outcome categories, the retained outcome (3ENR) is predicted most accurately, with 98.4 percent, whereas the other categories (1STOP [stopped out] and 2TRNF [transferred out]) are predicted with much less accuracy. Thus, the classification table allows us to evaluate a model based on its prediction accuracy and the cost of errors. In practice, the model could be improved by considering additional influential variables and interaction terms. More detailed information about the evaluation of this model using a separate validation sample is explained at the end of this section.

Neural Network. Neural networks were initially developed to solve problems similar to the way that biological nervous systems, such as the human brain, process information. This technique is composed of a large number of highly interconnected processing elements (neurons) working in parallel to solve specific problems (Dayhoff, 1990). In other words, several neurons arrange in layers to create a network with the ability to learn patterns and interrelationships of data.

According to Garson (1998), neural networks rely on the process for the hidden layer to perform the summation, and weights are constantly adjusted until an optimal threshold is reached, which then produces the outcome for a record. Neural networks are normally considered when the relationship between the influential variables and outcome is difficult to determine (Berry and Linoff, 1997).

Neural networks are self-adjusting. They are able to train themselves on a data set in order to construct a set of weights and a model for classification. The output of neural networks also contains a valuable sensitivity indicator that tells the relative importance of each variable in predicting the outcome. Despite this, care must be taken in their use because they require

Table 3.5. Classification Matrix for Prediction Accuracy by Multinomial Logistic Regression for Individual Students

Observed	Predicted			
	1STOP	2TRNF	3ENR	Percentage Correct
1STOP	19	4	36	32.2
2TRNF	8	18	73	18.2
3ENR	5	6	672	98.4
Overall percentage	3.8	3.3	92.9	84.3

considerable adjustment of the settings, such as the selection of topography and the setting of learning rates. Neural networks learn from example and cannot be programmed to perform a specific task. Thus, the examples must be selected carefully; otherwise, useful time will be wasted or, even worse, the network might function incorrectly (Ripley, 1995).

The relative importance of inputs from the generated neural network is shown in Figure 3.2, with the overall predicted accuracy of 83.9 percent. The input layer is made up of fourteen numerical fields (codes are explained in Table 3.4). In this network, there is one hidden layer containing three neurons, and the output layer contains three neurons corresponding to the three values of the retention outcome field. The input fields are listed in descending order of importance. Theoretically, the values would range from 0.0 to 1.0, with 1.0 being extremely important. In this network, college GPA at the end of the first year is the most important variable, followed by age and cumulative attempted units at the end of the first semester. The items "Fields," "Build Settings," and "Training Summary" contain technical details that will not be covered in this study.

Figure 3.3 shows the comparison of actual (rows) and predicted (columns) retention outcomes. The model predicts 98.3 percent of the retained outcome correctly but only 20.7 percent of transfer-out and 40.3 percent of stop-out outcomes. Thus, the matrix indicates that this model

Figure 3.2. Relative Importance of Inputs from the Generated Neural Net

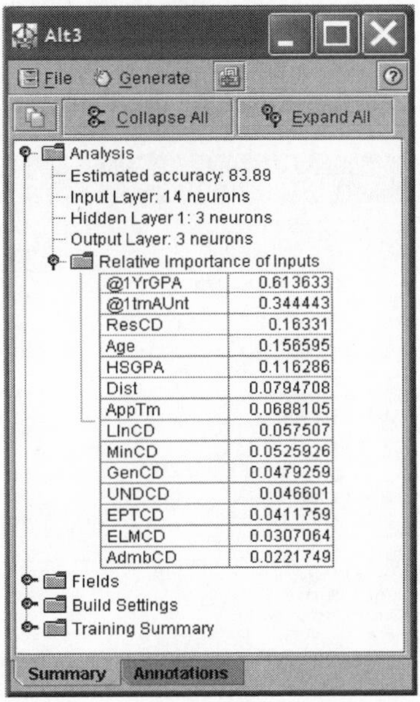

Figure 3.3. Neural Net Matrix of Actual and Predicted Retention Outcomes

Alt3		$N-Alt3 1STOP	2TRNF	3ENR
1STOP	Count	27	5	35
	Row %	40.299	7.463	52.239
2TRNF	Count	17	23	71
	Row %	15.315	20.721	63.964
3ENR	Count	8	4	679
	Row %	1.158	0.579	98.263

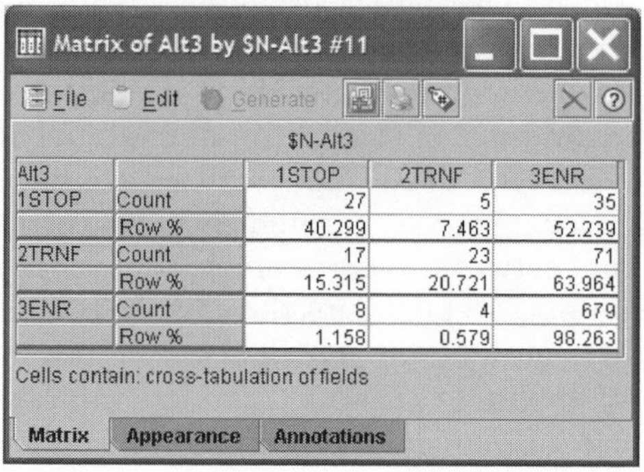

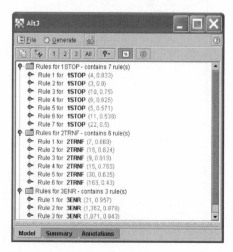

provides a reasonably accurate prediction of students who are more likely to be retained after one year with the institution.

C5.0 Rule Induction. This classification data-mining technique is referred to as the *rule induction* or *decision tree method*, which is able to cull through a set of influential variables by successively splitting a data set into subgroups on the basis of the relationships between influential variables and the outcome variable (Breiman, Friedman, Olshen, and Stone, 1984). Because the data set was recursively split into three retention outcomes and C5.0 works well with symbolic predictor variables, it was selected to create a rule induction model. Figures 3.4 and 3.5 show the results of C5.0 in the forms of a rule set and decision tree for predictions.

Figure 3.4. C5.0 Rules in the Rule Set Format

Figure 3.5. Unfolding a Branch of Stop-Out Outcome

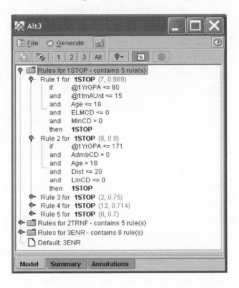

Figure 3.6 displays a decision tree that acts as an alternative format to help visualize the rule process. The root of the tree (far left side) shows the overall percentages and number of loaded records for all three retention outcomes. The first split is of the cumulative college GPA. The information from the bottom split indicates that if the first-year GPA is higher than 1.71, the outcome of retention is predicted to be over 87 percent or 632 students.

**Figure 3.6. Retained Outcome of First-Year GPA
in Decision Tree Format**

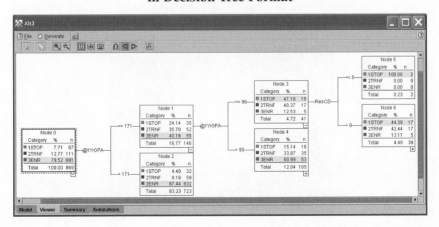

The advantage of using the C5.0 rule induction model over neural network is that the decision tree format clearly displays the influential variables that had an impact on the predicted field. However, unlike neural network, no sensitivity analysis is performed on the C5.0 model. The most important influential variables in the predictions can be thought of as those that divide the tree in its earliest stages (Lin, Loh, and Shih, 1997). Thus, in our example, the most important variable in predicting retention outcome is the first-year college GPA. This determination validates what was identified as the most "sensitive variable." Once the model divided the data into two groups (a GPA of 1.71 or higher and that of less than 1.71), it made predictions based on in-state residency, admission basis, and academic major.

Figure 3.7 shows the comparison of actual (rows) and predicted (columns) retention outcomes generated by the C5.0 modeling technique. The model predicts 99.0 percent of the retained outcome correctly but only 23.5 percent of stop-out and 30.1 percent of transfer-out outcomes. Similar to the results found from a neural network model, this C5.0 model provides a more accurate prediction of students who are more likely to be reenrolled after one year at the same institution.

Comparison of Overall Predictability. The model comparison is based on the same data used in the original model estimate. As discussed earlier, it is a common practice to evaluate models developed in the training data set using a separate validation sample.

When the prediction accuracy for training and validation data sets are compared, slight decreases are seen in predictability: –0.9 percent, –1.1 percent, and –1.8 percent for multinomial logistic regression, C5.0, and neural network, respectively, when the models were applied to the validation data. This implies that the training data and validation data are systematically similar. The multinomial logistic regression model is correct for 80.7 percent of validation data, which represents a drop from 81.6 percent found in the training data. Similarly, both C5.0 and neural network are correct for

Figure 3.7. C5.0 Matrix of Actual and Predicted Retention Outcomes

Matrix of Alt3 by $C-Alt3 #1

		$C-Alt3		
Alt3		1STOP	2TRNF	3ENR
1STOP	Count	28	4	87
	Row %	23.529	3.361	73.109
2TRNF	Count	7	61	135
	Row %	3.448	30.049	66.502
3ENR	Count	3	10	1240
	Row %	0.239	0.798	98.962

Cells contain: cross-tabulation of fields

84.4 percent and 82.1 percent, respectively, of the validation records, with a decrease of 85.5 percent and 83.9 percent, respectively, found in the training data. Thus, the overall results from validation data suggest that the C5.0 rule induction model is a slightly better model in predicting the first-year retention outcome of native students at this institution. However, because the other considerations, such as transparency of the model, could play a role in this analysis, caution should be used in selecting the best model.

Summary and Discussion

In higher education, studies of undergraduate retention are numerous and diverse in considering various combinations of academic, social, and financial factors (Berger and Braxton, 1998; Okun, Benin, and Brandt-Williams, 1996; Pascarella and Terenzini, 1980; St. John, 1994, 1996; Tinto, 1993). However, all of these studies combine the student's decision to reenroll as a binary yes-or-no decision because of a lack of information. According to McCormick and Carroll (1997), more than 25 percent of students who enter their postsecondary education at a four-year institution transfer to another. Therefore, with the NSC's and institutional data, the researchers could build models of retention with a practical alternative of transfer behavior.

This study examines the critical predictors influencing the decisions of first-time freshmen on completion of their first year using three predictive modeling techniques. From the overall analysis, the results suggest that the C5.0 rule induction model is a slightly better model than the other two in predicting the first-year retention outcome.

It is important that institutions consider using the appropriate predictive models described in this study in combination with other interventions to improve retention and graduation rates. This study focuses on a snapshot of leavers, but this needs to be accompanied by targeted studies of individual student cohorts. Thus, changing graduation rates with a long-standing retention problem has to be a multifaceted endeavor. One size of stop-out intervention does not fit all of those who leave, especially at large and diverse universities.

Successful retention programs that enhance student learning require changes not only in specific rules and incentives but also in campus, student, and parent culture. If the institution begins to expect more from students, students will in turn expect more from the university in various areas, such as campus residence; course access both on and off campus; prompt service of both during the day, in the evening, and on the weekends; and academic advising. Also, parents must be aware of the consequences of embracing the ethos that their children should pay for their college education themselves. Like medical treatment, institutions in higher education should manage successful retention and graduation initiatives by carefully isolating different influential factors behind leaving college and then tailor interventions that will directly target the root causes.

NEW DIRECTIONS FOR INSTITUTIONAL RESEARCH • DOI: 10.1002/ir

Future Research

This case study represents an initial attempt by a university to employ data-mining techniques. This effort has proved to be desirable and effective. However, more time is needed for the databases to be properly prepared for all future data-mining activities so that an automated process, such as data mining, will not suffer from inconsistent coding or incompatibility issues. Further, all three models have done well in predicting student transfer-out probability but less so with stopping out and retention.

Several methods may be attempted in future research. Cluster analysis may be attempted to create more homogeneous populations that may lend themselves to higher prediction accuracy. Boosting certain types of outcome records such as 1STOP and 2TRNF to better balance the overall presence of the outcomes may also increase the prediction accuracy.

References

Adelman, C. *Principal Indicators of Student Academic Histories in Postsecondary Education, 1972–2000*. Washington, D.C.: U.S. Department of Education, Institute of Education Sciences, 2004.

American College Test (ACT). "More First-Year College Students Return for Second Year; Fewer Students Graduate in Five Years." *ACT Newsroom,* Apr. 2001. http://www.act.org/news/releases/2001/04–26–01.html. Accessed June 9, 2004.

Berger, J. B., and Braxton, J. M. "Revising Tinto's Interactionalist Theory of Student Departure Through Theory Elaboration: Examining the Role of Organizational Attributes in the Persistence Process." *Research in Higher Education,* 1998, *39*(2), 103–119.

Berry, M.J.A., and Linoff, G. *Data Mining Technique: For Marketing, Sales, and Customer Support.* New York: Wiley Computer, 1997.

Breiman, L., Friedman, J. H., Olshen, R. A., and Stone, C. J. *Classification and Regression Trees.* Belmont, Calif.: Wadsworth, 1984.

Consortium for Student Retention Data Exchange (CSRDE). *AAUDE [Association of American Universities Data Exchange] Student Retention Report: 1992–1998 First-Time Freshmen Cohorts.* Norman: University of Oklahoma, Center for Institutional Data Exchange and Analysis, 2000.

Dayhoff, J. *Neural Network Architectures.* New York: Van Nostrand Reinhold, 1990.

Garson, G. D. *Neural Networks: An Introductory Guide for Social Scientists.* London: Sage, 1998.

Kleinbaum, D. G. *Logistic Regression: A Self-Learning Text.* New York: Springer-Verlag, 1994.

Learning Slope. *Policy Perspectives.* Philadelphia: Institute for Research on Higher Education, 1991.

Lin, T., Loh, W., and Shih, Y. "An Empirical Comparison of Decision Trees and Other Classification Methods." *Technical Report 979.* Madison: Department of Statistics, University of Wisconsin, 1997.

Luan, J. *Data Mining Essentials: Predictive Modeling and Clustering.* Aptos, Calif.: PRO Press, 2002.

McCormick, A. C., and Carroll, D. C. *Transfer Behavior Among Beginning Postsecondary Students: 1989–1994.* Washington, D.C.: U.S. Department of Education, National Center for Education Statistics, 1997.

National Student Clearinghouse. EnrollmentVerify, 2004. http://www.studentclearinghouse.org. Accessed Oct. 19, 2004.

Okun, M. A., Benin, M., and Brandt-Williams, A. "Staying in College: Moderators of the Relation Between Intention and Institutional Departure." *Journal of Higher Education,* 1996, *67*(5), 577–596.

Pascarella, E. T., and Terenzini, P. T. "Predicting Freshmen Persistence and Voluntary Dropout Decisions from a Theoretical Model." *Journal of Higher Education,* 1980, *51*(1), 60–75.

Ripley, B. D. *Pattern Recognition and Neural Networks.* New York: Cambridge University Press, 1995.

St. John, E. P. "The Influence of Student Aid on Within-Year Persistence by Traditional College-Age Students in Four-Year Colleges." *Research in Higher Education,* 1994, *35*(4), 455–480.

St. John, E. P. "The Nexus Between College Choice and Persistence." *Research in Higher Education,* 1996, *37*(2), 175–220.

Tinto, V. *Leaving College: Rethinking the Causes and Cures of Student Attrition.* (2nd ed.) Chicago: University of Chicago Press, 1993.

SUTEE SUJITPARAPITAYA is director of the Office of Institutional Research, California State University–Sacramento.

NEW DIRECTIONS FOR INSTITUTIONAL RESEARCH • DOI: 10.1002/ir

Data-mining technology's predictive modeling was applied to enhance the prediction of enrollment behaviors of admitted applicants at a large state university.

Applying Data Mining to Predict College Admissions Yield: A Case Study

Lin Chang

Although data-mining technologies have been applied widely and effectively in the business world, their use is relatively new to higher education. Data mining can be used to identify hidden patterns in data and extract actionable information for decision support, forecasts, and estimation. Combining domain knowledge of the business data with advanced techniques such as machine learning and artificial intelligence, data miners have been able to identify underlying relationships and features in data and generate models for better prediction. Traditional statistics with probability statements, though theoretically sound, can be limited and, at times, oversimplifying. Most hypothesis tests draw conclusions based on summary statistics, such as means or variances, rather than on individual uniqueness. Contrary to the myth, imprecision derived from classical statistics is actually commonplace. Using regression modeling as an example, the sizes of the confidence intervals drawn for individual cases can be much greater or wider than those drawn for the averages predicted by regression lines. On the other hand, by providing predictions at the individual level, data-mining technologies have higher degrees of granularity, which is becoming increasingly desirable in the institutional research field as institutions focus more and more on individual student–level prediction and attend to an almost infinite number of possible interrelationships of input variables.

NEW DIRECTIONS FOR INSTITUTIONAL RESEARCH, no. 131, Fall 2006 © Wiley Periodicals, Inc.
Published online in Wiley InterScience (www.interscience.wiley.com) • DOI: 10.1002/ir.187

The university under study had spent various resources in converting admitted students to enrolled students, understanding freshmen retention or six-year-completion trends, and evaluating program qualities. However, because of the complex and idiosyncratic nature, the effectiveness of enrollment management efforts had been difficult to evaluate. Data-mining techniques, by emphasizing individualized outcome prediction, seem promising in improving enrollment management in higher education (Luan, 2002).

This study shows how it is possible to apply data-mining technology and its predictive capability to further enhance the enrollment management strategies through increasing the understanding of admitted applicants. Admissions data were "mined" for hidden patterns. If hidden "gold nuggets" can be found, admissions yield may be explained and better predicted. As part of the data-mining demonstration, I compared the prediction accuracy from logistic regression, a more traditional statistical procedure, with those from two common data-mining techniques: neural networks and classification and regression tree (C&RT).

Research Questions

One of the major challenges that enrollment management professionals encounter in the admissions process is understanding why not all admitted students eventually enroll. As a matter of fact, from various institutional reports, admissions yield rates vary from institution to institution. A 100 percent admissions yield is not realistic. However, there appears to be an expected applicants-to-enrollment rate for various levels of institutions. Even though the need for increasing the yield may differ by institutions, the knowledge of who enrolls and why or who does not enroll and why not is always useful for admissions officers and university administrators. Answers to whether admitted students enroll randomly or whether certain groups of students enroll in certain institutions have significant implications for schools intent on increasing their admissions yield. Hidden yield patterns, if identified, can help redefine the target admission population. The information would also benefit recruitment activities, marketing and communication strategies, scholarship disbursement, program evaluation, and many areas of institutional policy and practices. In the context of the current study, based on the historical data of the university, about 45 percent of admitted students eventually matriculate.

This study seeks to answer the following questions:

1. Did admitted applicants enroll randomly without significant and identifiable patterns?
2. Are certain types or groups of admitted applicants more likely to enroll than others?
3. If the enrollment pattern could be identified and predictive models established, how well could future enrollment be predicted?

NEW DIRECTIONS FOR INSTITUTIONAL RESEARCH • DOI: 10.1002/ir

Data-Mining Methods

The data-mining study was conducted following the standard six-step data-mining procedure, cross-industry standard process (CRISP): business (or contextual) understanding, data understanding, data preparation, modeling, evaluation, and deployment.

Business Understanding. Studying admissions yields requires the insightful domain knowledge of enrollment management, admission process, and decision-making processes. In this university, less than half of the university's admitted applicants eventually enroll. Because the university plans to increase general enrollment by 10 percent, understanding its recruitment populations and their behavior patterns becomes necessary before predictive modeling work starts. Enrollment professionals at the university and presumably elsewhere often ponder the following questions: What makes admitted applicants enroll at this university? Which groups of applicants tend to enroll? Can the enrolled versus not-enrolled admitted applicants be distinguished in terms of demographic features (such as gender, ethnicity, or region), academic achievement (such as high school grade-point average [GPA], high school rank, scores on the American College Test [ACT] or Scholastic Assessment Test), university-specific strategies (such as recruitment activities, communication after students have been admitted, major programs), or scholarship offered? On obtaining answers to these questions, what methods and approaches can be adopted to increase the enrollment from the pool of admitted students? If patterns of enrollment can be identified and predicted, the university will be able to make better-informed decisions based on data for future recruitment efforts and budgeting purposes.

Data Understanding. In quantitative studies, answers to research questions rely on the availability of relevant data. At the same time, these studies are also limited by data. It is important to understand how and what information has been collected before data are mined. Admissions data at the studied institution were initially created using the Enrollment Management Action System (EMAS) based on student applications. EMAS data are exported regularly to the central Administrative Information System and updated and stored with enrollment information. The Admissions Office used the EMAS data system primarily for communication purposes. The system designed communication plans specific to individuals at various admission stages ranging from prospective applicants, inquirers, and official applicants to applicants being admitted or denied, registration-confirmed, and finally, enrolled. Various levels of data were collected at different admission stages. For example, minimal data could be collected for "prospects" by the institution. Available data of each admission stage are described below.

Prospects. This term refers to individuals with a good likelihood of applying and attending. One major data source of the university's prospects is a high school junior list from ACT. The state mandated that all public high school juniors take the ACT. In addition, the university obtains from

NEW DIRECTIONS FOR INSTITUTIONAL RESEARCH • DOI: 10.1002/ir

various sources lists of students with selected criteria of high school GPA or ACT scores along with lists of student names, high school graduation year, and self-reported GPAs. Lists of prospects were also established through a variety of university-initiated recruitment activities, such as high school visits, college fairs, senior-to-sophomore programs, other departmental recruiting programs, or purchased from ACT.

Inquirers. This category includes individuals who inquired or responded to information about the institution. The source of initial contacts includes walk-ins, telephone calls, the Internet, campus activities, and so on. Usually students' names and addresses are collected for this type of prospective applicant.

Applicants. Applicants refers to those who have applied for admission. At this stage, it is possible to collect complete information about the applicants.

Admitted. Applicants at this stage would receive an admission decision of being either admitted, denied, or pended for more information. Complete admissions data should have been collected for the admitted students.

Confirmed. This category refers to individuals who confirmed their future enrollment after being admitted. Not all admitted students respond with confirmation. Confirmed admitted applicants usually proceed to become enrolled students.

Enrolled. Individuals who enrolled on the first day of school were put into this category.

In general, a complete set of individual records would contain comprehensive information on demographic, academic, and communications activities of the applicants. Demographic fields include gender, ethnicity, age, region, domicile of origin (in state, out of state, or international), high school size, and so on. Academic factors include student's achievement before college: high school GPA, high school rank, ACT and SAT scores, and state-assigned admissions index scores—usually a combination of high school GPA and ACT or SAT score. Other academic factors include attempted programs, residency, student level, and degree or non-degree-seeking status. A maximum of fifteen communication activities with their corresponding dates, types (indicating how the information was communicated, such as through letter, mailing label, telecommunication, or e-mail), and names (describing the content) is recorded.

For the studied year 2003, the university's initial admissions file contained 26,611 records for the fall semester, where 50 percent stayed at the stage of prospects, 38 percent at the inquiry stage, and only about 12 percent applied, resulting in 2,849 being admitted as freshmen, transfers, or non-degree-seeking students. Because little information was collected for prospects and inquirers, records on prospects and inquirers were excluded from the analysis.

The university had a relatively high admissions rate, with more than 90 percent of the applicants being admitted. If the distribution of the outcome variable was not even, such as in this case where more than 90 percent of applicants were admitted, the data are considered "unbalanced." Some data-mining predictive modeling such as neural networks would respond poorly to unbalanced data. The chance of machine learning to make accurate predictions is greatly reduced with unbalanced data. Thus, the data were further filtered to include only admitted applicants for the initial analysis.

After the initial filtering, data quality was examined for the selected data set. The data-mining software provides a set of modules for the initial data check. Clementine has a unique strength in data preparation and transformation—a process important and fundamental to improving the quality of research. Without resorting to syntax writing, the process is a menu-driven, point-and-click approach that is flexible and user-friendly for nonprogrammers. Data-mining steps are carried through modules that are represented by icons or "nodes" on a "canvas." A "data audit" module (or node) is used for descriptive statistics by examining counts, means, standard deviations, minimums, and maximums. This node assisted the analysis with histograms that could be drilled down for a comprehensive "look" at the data. For example, by clicking on the histograms, detailed counts and percentages of that field are displayed. A "data quality" node evaluates data in terms of percentage of missing values. The data quality results indicate that some fields had a large number of missing values. For example, only 60 percent of admitted records had ACT scores or high school GPAs. However, not all missing values are truly missing. Some values are missing for legitimate reasons. Because ACT scores or high school GPAs are not required for transferred or non-degree-seeking students, they are usually not collected for transfer or nondegree applicants. The data quality check provides useful information about specific data fields of interest and how they were recorded. Knowledge gained through the data quality check facilitated the decision to further limit the scope of this study.

Other than missing values, the admitted applicants involved various groups with distinct characteristics, such as program level (graduate versus undergraduate students), degree-seeking status (degree-seeking versus non-degree-seeking students), or transfer status (freshmen versus transfer applicants). Different groups had different enrollment rates; for instance, almost all transfer students enrolled, and only about half of the admitted freshmen enrolled. Because of the missing values on important fields (ACT score or high school GPA) and the different enrollment rates (for transfer or freshmen applicants), the analysis was further confined to focusing on admitted freshmen alone. As a result, the target population was defined as the "admitted undergraduate degree-seeking freshmen." An additional advantage of this final target population was that the 40 to 45 percent freshmen admissions yield conveniently eliminated the potential problem of "unbalanced" data.

Data Preparation. After the target population was defined, the next step was to prepare an appropriate data set. Certain data fields (or variables) had to be combined or transformed, and only selected fields were mined. One example of combining and transforming data to new fields was from the communication records maintained at the university. Because EMAS was primarily for communication, individual communications between the university and students include records of the date, student name, and type of the communications. For the information to be useful, communication data were consolidated by type of communications (letter, e-mail, telephone, campus or student initiated, and so on). Each communication record was aggregated under each type of communication. As a result, new fields on each "type of communications" with frequencies were created.

The outcome variable was "enrollment status," indicating whether admitted students enrolled. Enrollment status was a dichotomous variable, coded 0 for not enrolled and 1 for enrolled. A list of predictors was carefully selected by the following rules. First, the chronological order of events was taken into consideration. Communication activities with students during their first semester or *after* their actual enrollment were excluded from the predictor list. Second, fields that provided redundant information were excluded. Only one field was kept for the analysis to prevent overpredicting. For example, the "registration confirmed" field was excluded as a predictor because it provides information almost identical to that in the enrolled field. The final selection of predictors include high school GPA, high school rank, high school size, SAT or ACT score, admissions index score, gender, ethnicity, age, region, domicile of origin, admission type, traditional or nontraditional status, major program, frequency of various types of communications, and sources of the initial contact.

The data set was then read and transformed onto a data-mining canvas where most of the procedures and model fitting took place. A wide selection of tools (called nodes) is at the disposal of data miners for "drawing" (that is, data analysis) on the canvas. Various clusters of nodes have different functions:

Sources nodes: algorithms used to read or import data from various databases such as SPSS or SAS

Record operation nodes: case management algorithms for selecting, merging, appending, counting distinct records, or sorting

Field operation nodes: algorithms for defining field types, reclassifying cases, deriving new files, partitioning, and converting rows to columns (Set-to-Flag)

Graphs nodes: algorithms for creating plots, displaying distributions and histograms, and evaluation graphs

Modeling nodes: the most crucial algorithms, which include clustering, predictive, and other data-mining models

Output nodes: algorithms for creating various reports such as data quality, statistics, analysis, and data outputs including SPSS, SAS, EXCEL, and SQL exports.

NEW DIRECTIONS FOR INSTITUTIONAL RESEARCH • DOI: 10.1002/ir

A set of field- and record-operation nodes similar to syntax modules in the Statistical Package for the Social Sciences (SPSS) software was used to transform variable fields and selected and aggregate cases. After the admissions data were read, some fields were recoded into simpler and more meaningful groupings. For example, existing state and county codes were combined to form a "region" code using the "derive" node and its "formula" function, similar to the "compute" command in SPSS or the Statistical Analysis System. Another field, the original long (more than 150) list of "initial source of contact," was consolidated into fewer categories. The "set-a-flag" node was used to create dummy variables in combining and transforming the communication activities field. As mentioned earlier, to determine the effect of the number of communication activities on enrollment, new flag fields were created for each nonblank communication field. The resulting frequency of communication activities was simply the sum of those flags. The rate of missing values was periodically examined using the "quality" node. Outcomes of the analyses were examined using the "table" or "matrix" output nodes. An example of the data-mining stream is shown in Figure 4.1. Demographic information—gender, ethnicity, and region—and average academic performance on high school GPA and ACT composite scores are listed in Tables 4.1, 4.2, and 4.3.

Figure 4.1. A Data-Mining Stream Canvas

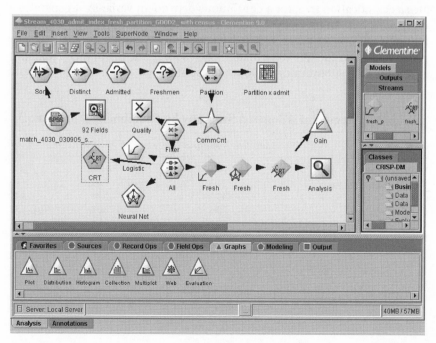

Table 4.1. Ethnicity of Admitted Students by Enrollment Status and Gender (no.)

	Admitted Not Enrolled		Enrolled		
Ethnicity	Female	Male	Female	Male	Total
Native American	14	6	7	7	34
African American	37	18	25	12	92
Asian	29	25	8	12	74
Hispanic	117	79	92	65	353
Caucasian	346	274	226	200	1,046
Foreign	10	39	5	8	62
Unknown	10	11	12	8	41
Total	563	452	375	312	1,702

Modeling. Although more than a dozen modeling nodes were available in Clementine, three predictive modelings were used for the study: C&RT, neural networks, and logistic regression.

First, the study used C&RT to develop classification systems that predict or later classify future observations based on a set of decision rules. The C&RT method is based on minimization of impurity measures: a node is considered "pure" if 100 percent of the cases in the node fall into a similar category of the target field. For a categorical outcome field, C&RT generates a classification tree; for a continuous dependent variable, it generates a regression tree. In this study, because the target is categorical, a classification or decision tree was generated, as shown in Figure 4.2.

All splits in the tree were binary. Each subsample (or branch) was split again until the subsamples could not be split anymore. Obviously, it would

Table 4.2. Region of Admitted Students by Enrollment Status (no.)

Region	Admitted Not Enrolled	Enrolled	Total
Local	144	289	433
Nearby region in state	240	178	418
Other in state	350	149	499
Out of state	108	24	132
WUE state	124	34	158
Foreign	49	13	62
Total	1,015	687	1,702

Note: WUE = Western Undergraduate Exchange, a program of the Western Interstate Commission for Higher Education (WICHE). Through WUE, students in western states may enroll in many two-year and four-year college programs at a reduced rate of 150 percent of the institution's regular resident tuition. WUE tuition is considerably lower than nonresident tuition.

NEW DIRECTIONS FOR INSTITUTIONAL RESEARCH • DOI: 10.1002/ir

Table 4.3. Academic Achievement of Freshmen by Enrollment Status

| Academic Achievement | Admitted Not Enrolled | | | Enrolled | | |
	Index	High School GPA	ACT	Index	High School GPA	ACT
Scores	95.58	2.98	20.48	93.11	2.99	19.93
Count	959	1,002	862	648	665	624

not be useful if a model contained rules applied to each individual record. Unless the split distinguishes groups of cases, the lowest-level rules usually would not generalize well. Thus, lower-level splits often are discarded or "pruned" by settings under model specifications (Figure 4.3).

The second modeling node used in the study was the neural networks model, also called a "multilayer perceptron." It was used to create neural networks that simulate, in a simplified way, how human brains would process information.

As the model in Figure 4.4 shows, the neural networks had three layers: an input layer, some hidden layers, and an output layer (in this case, it is "enrollment status"). Neural network had the reputation of being a "black box." The process in which it analyzes data was through the hidden layers that communicate with both the input and output variables. It thus forms

Figure 4.2. A Decision Tree

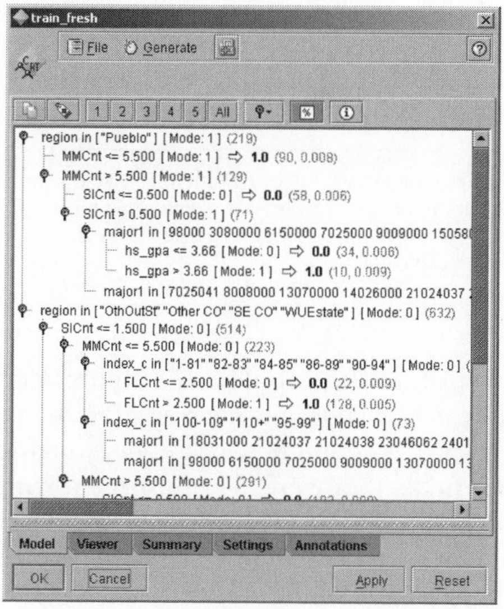

Figure 4.3. A Rule Set

Rules for 1 — contains 4 rule(s)
    Rule 1 for 1.0 (90, 0.815)
        if MMCnt ≤ 5
        and region = Pueblo
        then 1.00
    Rule 2 for 1.0 (30, 0.812)
        if act_read > 17
        and SICnt > 1
        and region = SE CO
        then 1.000
    Rule 3 for 1.0 (18, 0.8)
        if CommCnt ≤ 9
        and SICnt ≤ 1
        and region = SE CO
        then 1.000
    Rule 4 for 1.0 (51, 0.717)
        if gender = F
        and FLCnt ≤ 5
        and MMCnt > 5
        and region = Pueblo
        then 1.000
Rules for 0 — contains 5 rule(s)
    Rule 1 for 0.0 (100, 0.814)
        if region = OthOutSt
        then 0.000
    Rule 2 for 0.0 (85, 0.782)
        if region = WUEstate
        then 0.000
        ....

Note: MMCnt = Mass mailing materials; SICnt = Student-initiated communication; CommCnt = Total count of communication; SE CO = Southeast region of Colorado; F = Female; FLCnt = Letters to students; OthOutSt = Other out of state; WUEstate = Western Undergraduate Exchange states as defined in note for Table 4.2.

complex relationships between inputs and outputs and makes expressing them mathematically in one equation, such as a logistic regression equation, impossible. Each layer in a neural network node contained units representing input or output fields that were also connected with varying weights. The network examined individual records, generated a prediction for each record, and made adjustments to the weights. The process was repeated many times until one or more of the stopping criteria (set by the user or system default), such as percentage accuracy, or time (minutes), had been met.

NEW DIRECTIONS FOR INSTITUTIONAL RESEARCH • DOI: 10.1002/ir

Figure 4.4. A Neural Network Analysis

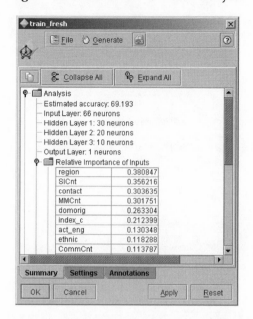

The third approach employed logistic regression modeling to illustrate that traditional statistics still had a place in data mining. As a commonly used and understood statistical approach, the logistic regression model was applied in this study to compare and contrast with the solutions derived from C&RT and neural network.

Evaluation. All three approaches have included an evaluation procedure. The target population, admitted undergraduate degree-seeking freshmen, was partitioned randomly into two data sets, training and testing. The training data set was used to develop the model, and the testing group was to validate the model developed by the training data set before the final model could be applied to current data (called *scoring*). All models produced predictions for individual students based on learning the patterns and rules of existing records with known outcomes. Model fitting involved many reiterations between training and testing data sets as well as several model-evaluation processes.

In addition, prediction results were also evaluated in several ways. An "analysis" node produced the probability of correct versus wrong predictions by each model. Through the "coincidence" or "confusion" matrix (Figure 4.5), a 2 × 2 table with rows defined by actual values and columns defined by predicted values, the number of hits or misses by each predictive model was evaluated and compared.

The study also evaluated the predictions from the three modeling nodes by examining their level of agreements. The number of cases predicted by

Figure 4.5. Coincidence Matrix from the Analysis Node

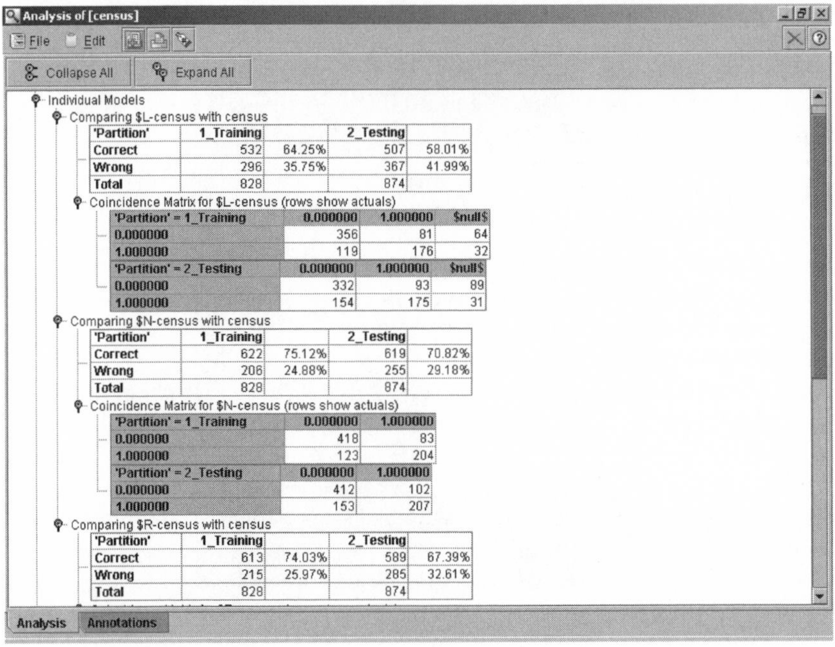

Analysis of [census]

File   Edit

Collapse All   Expand All

Individual Models

Comparing $L-census with census

'Partition'	1_Training		2_Testing	
Correct	532	64.25%	507	58.01%
Wrong	296	35.75%	367	41.99%
Total	828		874	

Coincidence Matrix for $L-census (rows show actuals)

'Partition' = 1_Training	0.000000	1.000000	$null$
0.000000	356	81	64
1.000000	119	176	32
'Partition' = 2_Testing	0.000000	1.000000	$null$
0.000000	332	93	89
1.000000	154	175	31

Comparing $N-census with census

'Partition'	1_Training		2_Testing	
Correct	622	75.12%	619	70.82%
Wrong	206	24.88%	255	29.18%
Total	828		874	

Coincidence Matrix for $N-census (rows show actuals)

'Partition' = 1_Training	0.000000	1.000000
0.000000	418	83
1.000000	123	204
'Partition' = 2_Testing	0.000000	1.000000
0.000000	412	102
1.000000	153	207

Comparing $R-census with census

'Partition'	1_Training		2_Testing	
Correct	613	74.03%	589	67.39%
Wrong	215	25.97%	285	32.61%
Total	828		874	

Analysis   Annotations

the nodes that were the same (agreed) by all three nodes was the test of agreements conducted by the study.

Coincidence matrices from the analysis output are shown in Figure 4.5 for all three predictive models, with L indicating logistic regression, R classification and regression tree, and N neural network. Individual models varied in their performances. Agreements between the three models were 66 percent; of those, 82 percent agreed with the actual enrollment.

Results from the model building seemed to suggest that admitted students did not enroll randomly at the studied institution and, to a certain degree, their enrollment decision could be predicted. A reasonably large portion of student enrollment could be accurately predicted by several predictive models. The probability of correct prediction from C&RT, neural network, and logistic regression models was about 74 percent, 75 percent, and 64 percent, respectively, supported by results from the corresponding testing groups: 67 percent, 71 percent, and 58 percent.

Rule sets generated by C&RT showed that local students and students of certain score ranges tended to enroll. Predictions were determined by factors or interactions of factors such as region, communication type and frequency, degree major, and admissions index score. Based on the numbers and percentages associated with each "tree split," an enrollment prediction was made. In general, local students with student-initiated communications tended to enroll. Then, at the next layer, if those students applied for a certain degree major, they would be more likely to enroll. Further predictions were represented by more tree splits.

Similar results were described by the list of the relative importance of input factors through neural networks, where region, communication types, and certain sources of contact were most important. The logistic regression model also showed that region and contact sources were important predictors for enrollment (see Table 4.4). The table shows the reduction in the –2 log likelihood function as variables are added to the logistic regression model. This is a measure of the overall fit of the model.

The various models were also evaluated graphically. Three graph nodes were employed by this case study. When the predicted value accurately matched the actual value, it was called a *hit*. The "gains chart" (Figure 4.6) showed the proportion of total hits that occurred in each quantile. Other gauges were quartiles, quintiles, or percentiles. Gains were computed as (number of hits ÷ total number of hits) ÷ 100 percent. For a model to be considered good, the cumulative gains chart would rise steeply toward 100 percent and then level off.

The "baseline" and the "best line" could be displayed for most plots. The baseline always indicates a completely random distribution of hits where the model prediction is irrelevant, and the best line indicates 100 percent hits. The gains chart for the three predictive models and their baselines and best lines are shown in Figure 4.6. The "gains" seemed to indicate that as the number of cases increased, the C&RT model performed the best.

Table 4.4. A Logistic Regression Model Showing a Step Summary

Model	Action	Effect(s)	Model Fitting Criteria	Effect Selection Tests		
			–2 Log Likelihood	χ^{2a}	df	Significance
0	Entered	Intercept	881.278			
1	Entered	region	804.516	75.143	4	.000
2	Entered	MMCnt	771.082	32.586	1	.000
3	Entered	SICnt	753.104	17.988	1	.000
4	Entered	contact	733.558	18.892	7	.009
5	Entered	act_read	724.766	8.705	1	.003

Note: The stepwise method used is forward entry.
[a]The chi-square for entry is based on the score test.

**Figure 4.6. Gains Chart for C&RT (R), Neural Network (N),
and Logistic Regression (L)**

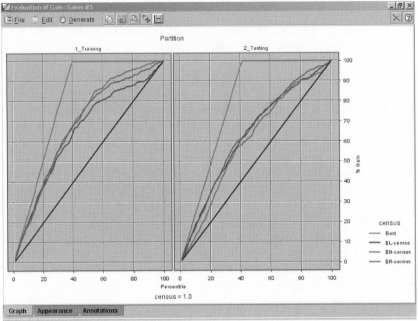

Two more types of charts were also examined by the authors, but because of their complexity, the graphs are not included. The "lift chart" represented the percentage of records in each quantile that were hits with the overall percentage of hits:

(Hits in Quantile ÷ Records in Quantile) ÷ (Total Hits ÷ Total Records)

For a good model, the cumulative lift chart should start the ratio of hits well above 1.0 and remain at a high level. A line around 1.0 horizontally indicates that the model provides no information.

The "profit chart" represented the revenue for each record minus the cost for the record:

Sum of Revenue for Records in Quantile
– Sum of Costs for Records in Quantile

Profits and costs could be fixed or defined. The cumulative profit chart showed the sum of profits as the number of cases within the sample increases. For a good model, profits would show a well-defined peak somewhere in the middle. A straight line indicates that no information was provided by the model. As a result, all charts reflected a similar evaluation on the three predictive models. Overall, the data-mining models, C&RT and neural network, performed better than the logistic regression model. When validated using the testing data set, all three models performed better than the baseline, indicating that all three models provided more information than mere guessing.

Deployment. To see how models performed in the real world, predictions based on models developed from a previous year's data were compared and evaluated with the actual enrollment at the later year (for example, fall 2003 versus fall 2004). Even though models achieved 75 percent prediction accuracy while validated by the other half of data from the same year, results indicated that in predicting for the actual enrollment for the next year, the prediction accuracy was reduced to 64 percent. Some possible explanations for the reduced prediction rate were that the university raised its admissions index scores, changed its name during the study period, and had several program changes between the two years. To be useful, predictive models should continue to be developed with updated data.

Overall, information provided by successful models was useful in several ways. First, knowledge developed for predictions among applicants who may or may not enroll could prompt future communication plans to be tailored to facilitate enrollment while recruiting. Second, future recruitment activities and associated budgets could be evaluated and redirected toward targeted populations identified by the data-mining models. Third, knowledge related to degree majors learned from the data-mining models could be informative to university administrators or academic officers in reviewing academic programs.

Data-mining technology was a process for continuous improvement. Predictive models can be modified periodically by bringing in new factors so that the models stay adaptive and continue to be useful for future applications. For example, in this study, one of the factors that should be accounted for is the financial aid information. Because of the nature of financial aid processing at the university, initial offers were overwritten by later updates; therefore, complete data were not available for this study. Plans are being developed to include financial aid data in future follow-ups.

Conclusions

A major difference between data-mining predictive modeling and conventional statistical modeling is that data mining–based predictive models can make predictions for individual records using complex sets of rules whereas classical statistical models do best drawing general conclusions about average and group means. Both approaches have their advantages and disadvantages. Conventional statistics will continue to have great value in testing group differences. Classical hypothesis testing and probability statements with confidence intervals are conceptually informative yet often not practical in making individual decisions. Data-mining applications are aimed at tackling individual-based clustering and predictive modeling that often interact with a live data warehouse, and the outcomes can be immediately applied to real-time data.

This case study has shown that data-mining predictive models, C&RT or neural networks, generated better solutions than the traditional logistic regression in predicting admissions yield in a large higher education institution. On the surface, data-mining models may appear to be nontheoretical and unconventional, but the models in this study proved that results were actionable and practical and, thus, highly desirable to enrollment professionals. Because of its practical features, data-mining technology not only has been widely applied in the business world but also has a lot of potential in higher education. By providing practical results, institutional researchers can better inform teaching and learning activities and assist university administrators with data-supported decision making.

Reference

Luan, J. "Data Mining and Its Applications in Higher Education." In A. M. Serban and J. Luan (eds.), *Knowledge Management: Building a Competitive Advantage in Higher Education*. New Directions for Institutional Research, no. 113. San Francisco: Jossey-Bass, 2002.

LIN CHANG *is director of institutional research and analysis at Colorado State University–Pueblo.*

NEW DIRECTIONS FOR INSTITUTIONAL RESEARCH • DOI: 10.1002/ir

5

This case study documents a successful application of data-mining techniques in enrollment management through a partnership between the admissions office, a business administration master's-degree program, and the institutional research office at Willamette University (Salem, Oregon).

Expanding the Role of Institutional Research at Small Private Universities: A Case Study in Enrollment Management Using Data Mining

Christopher M. Antons, Elliot N. Maltz

Most private institutions depend heavily on tuition income to fund operations. Therefore, enrollment management is essential to fiscal planning. Specifically, the admissions offices must accurately project two key financial indicators: yield and discount rate.

An institution's yield is the percentage of admitted students who will actually enroll. If a yield is overestimated, fewer-than-expected students will enroll, and university revenue will decrease. If the yield is underestimated, too many students will enroll, in which case the class size may exceed the fixed capacity, resulting in significant incremental costs for additional housing, faculty, and other resources. Overenrollment could compromise the quality of instruction as classrooms become overcrowded and student-to-faculty ratios exceed the level conducive to optimal learning.

The discount rate is the projected financial aid to be allocated to students as a percentage of tuition. All universities offer financial aid to a large proportion of their incoming students, both as a means of meeting students' financial need and as a recruiting tool. Financial aid allocations provide a powerful lever for admissions, but these decisions have major fiscal implications as well. If too much financial aid is allocated, a university may be gaining too many students whose tuition and fees do not cover the actual costs of their education, therefore putting a financial strain on the institution.

Because the actual ratio of admitted students to enrolled students is not known in advance, a critical task for any admissions office is to accurately estimate yields and discount rates each year. Some schools utilize the institutional research office to perform the task. Others equip their admissions office with statistical experts (Bontrager, 2004). However, for smaller schools, because of limited resources, individual administrative offices are typically thinly staffed. Neither the admissions nor institutional research offices have enough staff to adequately perform the statistical modeling tasks on top of all the other responsibilities their personnel have to shoulder. In this case, the admissions office used an outside consultant to build an enrollment model for predicting these key metrics.

This approach has a number of serious drawbacks. First, because the model built by the consultant is often proprietary, the admissions office has limited knowledge and little control over the model development. Thus, institutional learning about how and why admitted students actually enroll is seriously limited. Second, the models are usually built on global assumptions that apply to all of the institutions for which the consultant provides services. Thus, the model may not incorporate the idiosyncratic differences of individual institutions. Finally, the admissions process has become much more capricious in recent years due to the increased sophistication of applicants. These prospective students are likely to research and apply to multiple institutions over varying time periods (Galoti and Mark, 1994; Hossler, Schmit, and Vesper, 1999). This leads to a transient application pool. Thus, the statistical analysis performed by an outside agency is limited in how it can adapt to an ever-changing admissions process.

This case study illustrates an emerging solution of using institutional resources outside the department of institutional research for the development of in-house models based on data-mining tools. Specifically, we describe a partnership among the Willamette University (Salem, Oregon) Admissions Office, a data-mining class for a master's degree in business administration (MBA), and the Institutional Research Office to develop an effective model to predict yield and discount rates and an interface for managers to apply the model to improve enrollment management.

The next three sections provide an overview of the process whereby the model and tool were developed, followed by a discussion of the results of using the model and tool. In the final section are discussed key lessons learned from the partnership effort and potential enhancement to the enrollment management process.

Genesis of a Partnership

The process described below was developed at Willamette University, a small liberal arts college in the Northwest. In addition to the College of Liberal Arts (CLA), the university has an MBA program. Traditionally, the Admissions Office at the CLA has hired an outside consultant to estimate total

NEW DIRECTIONS FOR INSTITUTIONAL RESEARCH • DOI: 10.1002/ir

yield using traditional statistical models. This approach had led to impre-
cise estimates of both yield and discount rate and ultimately significant
declines in actual revenue accruing from tuition over the past three years.

About this time, an MBA professor teaching a course on data mining
was looking for a real-life data set for his students to gain practical insights
into the data-mining process. He approached the vice president for enrollment to see if she would release data associated with the enrollment process
to the students. Because the most pressing need of the university was to
develop more useful models for predicting yield for the CLA, they agreed
to a joint project by pooling resources and employing faculty and students
from the MBA program and administrative personnel from admissions and
institutional research offices.

The students in the data-mining class started to work on developing a
predictive model under the guidance of the data-mining professor with
inputs from institutional research and the Admissions Office. The end result
would be a tool that the admissions and institutional research staff could
use in a timely manner to make admissions decisions designed to improve
or maintain enrollment yield while reducing financial aid costs.

This collaborative approach seemed to offer a number of advantages to
the Admissions Office. First, because the data analysis is conducted on campus, the Admissions Office has full control over how often the modeling is
updated; its management staff can spend a significant amount of time
acquainting the MBA student team with the unique admissions process used
at the school. Thus, the modeling process would be customized for the university. In addition, the institutional research staff can also provide insightful input into the modeling process.

The data-mining approach offers additional advantages. First, because
in data mining the students do not approach the modeling process with any
preconceived notion of the key variables to be included in the model, new
insights are often provided to the Admissions Office that would not have
emerged with the models typically used by consultants. Second, data-
mining models such as cluster analysis, decision trees, and neural networks
are designed to deal with large amounts of variables and the interactions
among them. This also gives new insights that would have often been overlooked by traditional approaches. The combination of the intense interaction between the student team, the Admissions Office, and the institutional
research staff and data-mining approaches maximized institutional knowledge acquisition. As such, the estimates of yield and discount rate would
become more precise as the program became more advanced.

Applying Data Mining to the Admissions Process

Data mining is an iterative process of finding trends and patterns in data
(Groth, 2000). The objective of this process is to sort through large quanti-
ties of data and discover new information. In this case, the students followed

the procedure for data-mining projects: the Cross Industry Standard Procedures for Data Mining (CRISP-DM) (Chapman and others, 2000). The CRISP-DM procedure, depicted in Figure 5.1, suggests six steps to developing successful data-mining models: institutional understanding, data understanding, data preparation, modeling, evaluation, and deployment (see Exhibit 5.1 for a broader description of these steps). The students closely followed these steps.

Project Goals. The institutional-understanding phase began with discussions to clearly articulate goals for the data-mining project. Specifically, the goal is that by the beginning of year three, the graduate school of management would develop a yield management model that would

1. Reduce the range of errors in yield estimates from the pool of admitted students
2. Increase the Admissions Office understanding of the factors that induced students to come to the university

Figure 5.1. The CRISP Paradigm

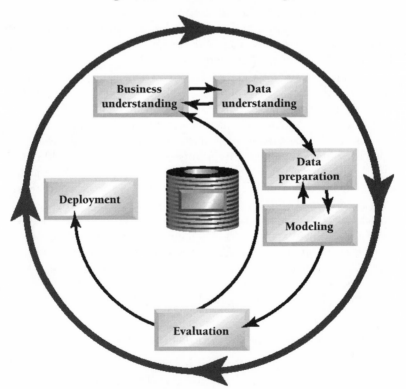

Exhibit 5.1. The CRISP Method

1. *Institutional Understanding.* Generating a clear understanding between the analyst and the manager as to

- The current situation
- The goals of the data-mining project
- The resources available for the project, both human and material

2. *Data Understanding.* In this phase

- Data sources are identified and described in terms of fields, records, and formats available
- Raw data are collected from the appropriate sources
- Initial data exploration is conducted to get a "feel" for the data, including generating basic statistics, identifying duplicate and incomplete fields, and generating initial hypotheses

3. *Data Preparation.* The data are put into a form that is appropriate for the modeling process, which includes

- Selecting the actual data to be used in the analysis from the sources identified during the data-understanding phase
- Combining data sets where necessary to create a single file for analysis
- Documenting why data were included or excluded
- Cleaning the data of duplicate fields or records and creating suitable identifiers for missing data
- Creating new variables based on existing raw data to make the data accessible to the models being considered or that are representative of the initial hypotheses proposed (or both)
- Creating a training data set used to develop or modify hypotheses and a validation data set used to validate the final model created based on the training set

4. *Modeling.* In this part of the process, the analyst chooses and runs the model(s) on the training data set to address the managerial objective(s) identified in the institutional-understanding phase. In choosing the models, the following must be considered:

- Which technique(s) are appropriate for the management objective(s)
- Which outputs managers using the models can and will use
- What technical and data constraints are faced in this project

In running the models, managers must consider the following:

- What is an acceptable final result from an analytical standpoint?
- What is an acceptable result from a managerial standpoint?
- Which models will be used as input to the final model, and which model results will be output to the managers?

5. *Evaluation.* The final model developed in the modeling phase is run on the validation set to determine if the result is purely data driven or can be generalized to a broader population. In this phase, the following must be determined:

New Directions for Institutional Research • DOI: 10.1002/ir

- Whether the results on the validation set are consistent with those obtained for the training set
- If they are not consistent, what does this mean from a managerial standpoint?
- Do the results provide an acceptable solution that can guide managerial actions? If the results are deemed managerially acceptable, then move to deployment (step 6). If they are not acceptable, then return to one of the previous steps to refine the models or abandon the project.

6. *Deployment.* The analyst takes the data-mining results and develops a strategy for using the results to address the issues identified in the institutional-understanding phase. The deployment strategy could be

- Creating software to be used by managers to address the issue of interest
- Producing report(s) to be used by the appropriate managers
- Presenting the results to the appropriate managers

---

3. Be the basis of a management tool that the staff in the Admissions Office could use to manage the yield and discount rate more effectively and respond to other strategic initiatives introduced by the president, the trustees of the institution, or both.

Year One. During the initial two-month period, significant time investment was required from both admissions and institutional research staff to ensure that the developers of the model and tool (that is, members of the data-mining class) thoroughly understood the data available and the desired outcomes.

The next six months were devoted to establishing a database amenable to analysis using the advanced data-mining tools. The admissions and institutional research staff were continually involved in this stage to ensure that the data were delivered in a form adequate for further analysis. Although the time costs were significant, one of the benefits to the administrative personnel was that as they worked with the students, they became more comfortable managing the information process on which these models were developed.

The developers of the models were guided by admissions professionals but not bound by their advice. The project required using data that had not been typically utilized by the Admissions Office. The students combined data from different sources within the university. It is important to note that one potential benefit of such a partnership is that the final model will likely use variables that may not have been considered by an outside consultant or possibly even statistical professionals in the Institutional Research Office.

The data were prepared in time for introduction in the spring semester of 2002 for the students to begin their analysis. The students, guided by the faculty member and the admissions staff, spent four months analyzing the previous three years (2000–2002) of admissions data to develop a model that would predict the overall yield of the admitted pool and predict whether any individual student within the pool would actually enroll at the university.

The models were evaluated over the summer period based on actual enrollees. In addition, during the summer period a small student team developed a user-friendly software interface that allowed the admissions personnel to utilize the models with minimal understanding of their underlying mathematical properties.

It soon became clear that the model developed by the students predicted overall enrollment with the same level of accuracy as the outside consultant. In addition, it provided a number of additional insights. Further, the model had the ability to predict any individual applicant's likelihood of enrolling, and this offered the opportunity to better manage the discount rate when managing the 2004 pool of admitted students.

The iterative modeling and evaluation process used in data mining allowed for a more useful model and interface than that offered by the consultant. Importantly, the evaluation of year one provided a number of important insights for the continuation of the project in year two. For instance, some of the variables included in the model suggested new variables to include in the database for the next year's analysis. In addition, the admissions staff suggested that future analysis also provide a set of models that would place equal weight on predicting both enrollees and nonenrollees.

Year Two. As shown in Figure 5.2, the second year began with a discussion of the lessons learned from the first year and ways to revise the database based on these lessons. A number of variables were introduced into the new databases, and some of the existing variables were reformatted to make

Figure 5.2. The CRISP Process Applied to the Admissions Project

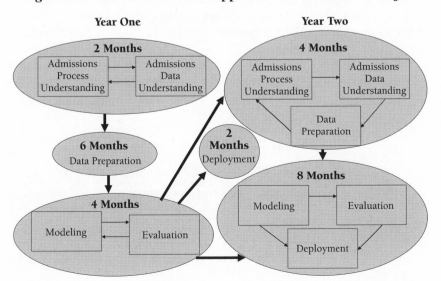

the modeling process more efficient. The total amount of time devoted to understanding the admissions process and formatting the data dropped from eight months to four months.

During this period, the admissions personnel, in conjunction with the institutional research personnel, began using the models and interfaces developed in the first year. As noted earlier, the institutional goals were to create an admissions pool from the 2003 applicants that would result in an incoming class in 2004 with a lower discount rate while maintaining the quality of the actually enrolled students.

Model Development Process. The data-mining team used the Clementine software package from SPSS, Inc., during the modeling phase of the project. The modeling phase actually began with the development of data-driven scenarios. This is depicted in Figure 5.3 as the data exploration phase.

During the exploration phase, the full set of cleaned data (2000–2003 admissions) was used to identify highly correlated variables using plots and correlation matrices and cluster analysis. In terms of highly correlated variables, the team was specifically concerned with variables that were correlated with whether an admitted student would actually choose to attend. In terms of the highly correlated records, the team was looking for large groups with similar characteristics that also, as a group, seemed to have an unusually high or unusually low propensity to attend. When these groups were found, flag variables were created to allow such group membership information to be included in the model.

The team then split the full data set into two randomly selected data sets, a training data set and a validation data set. The training set was used to develop a logistic regression model for deployment. Logistic regression is similar to linear regression, which was well understood by institutional research personnel but is necessary when the dependent variable is dichotomous. From a managerial perspective, it would be most useful to deploy a logistic regression model.

To generate the logistic regression model, the team began by taking into account a wide range of variables: all the variables suggested by the enroll-

Figure 5.3. Modeling Process

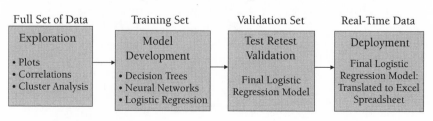

Full Set of Data	Training Set	Validation Set	Real-Time Data
Exploration • Plots • Correlations • Cluster Analysis	Model Development • Decision Trees • Neural Networks • Logistic Regression	Test Retest Validation Final Logistic Regression Model	Deployment Final Logistic Regression Model: Translated to Excel Spreadsheet

ment management personnel as important or managerially relevant, new variables that had been identified as potentially important in year one, and additional variables identified in the exploration phase described above in a number of decision tree and neural network models. This was to identify

- Variables that could be deleted from the final logistic regression model
- Additional variables that might be included as main effects in the logistic regression model
- Interaction effects that should be included in the model

After thorough analysis of the decision trees and neural network models, the suggested main and interaction effects were included in a preliminary logistic regression model. Successive regression models were developed and tested. The final model increased the predictive precision of the model, particularly in predicting those who actually enrolled.

The final model was submitted to validation using the validation data set. The purpose of test-retest is to determine if the models built in the training data set would be generalized to other sets of data. The results were consistent with those obtained from the training data set. The same variables in the training data set were significant in the validation data set, and the predictive accuracies were similar. Therefore, the model was ready for deployment.

The model was deployed using an Excel spreadsheet. Inputting the actual data values to the parameter fields allowed the model to display the expected results at individual, group, and overall levels. This allowed both institutional research and enrollment management personnel to use the final model with great flexibility and convenience.

Results. A final model using real-time data correctly classified the enrollment disposition of 66 percent of admitted applicants for the 2004 admissions cycle while maintaining the correct classification of enrollees to over 49 percent and nonenrollees to over 78 percent. The set of predictors included entrance scores, high school grade point average, geographical origin, and financial need amount of applicants as well as grant, scholarship, and loan amounts in the financial aid package. The model was, therefore, sensitive to changes in the financial aid packages as well as quality and geographical distributions.

The application tool allowed the enrollment management staff to modify financial aid amounts and calculate an expected probability of enrollment correspondingly based on changing values of the financial aid. The Institutional Research Office then worked with the enrollment management staff to identify a set of scenarios based on differing financial aid packages for groups of admitted applicants. Expected yields and expected net tuition were then computed for each scenario. After several iterations, the enrollment management staff settled on a financial aid package that resulted in the desired enrollment yield and net tuition income.

Supplementary Models

The insights provided during the data-mining process spurred additional statistical analysis by institutional research. In the 2004 admissions cycle, the staff applied data-mining models to update predicted probabilities of enrollment based on a changing admitted pool and revised institutional aid packages. Specifically, the model to predict the overall yield based on a prior year's data was applied to the 2003 applicant pool under changing financial aid packaging policies.

The computation of individual probabilities of enrolling provided by the interface allowed for estimates of enrollment; financial aid cost and resulting net tuition revenue; and profiles of predicted entering students with respect to academic qualifications, geography, and ethnic diversity. After each iteration, predicted yields, aid costs, net revenue, and profiles were recomputed.

Information about probabilities of enrolling for groups of applicants with varying academic qualifications and financial need allowed the enrollment management staff to shape the award of aid without negatively affecting expected yield.

Decisions about aid packaging were then applied to the 2004 pool of admitted students. The process did not alter admissions decisions but altered decisions about financial aid. Probabilities of enrolling were then computed on the 2004 admitted pool, and similarly, estimates of enrolling, financial aid cost and net tuition revenue, and profiles of expected enrollees were obtained. With new information obtained about financial need, estimates were updated throughout the admissions cycle.

In addition to better estimating admissions yield, predictions at the individual level allowed better estimates of expected revenue from the incoming class as well as profiling with respect to academic qualities, geography, and ethnic diversity. In summary, the data-mining tools allowed the university to rapidly reestimate the impact of enrollment management decisions and plan for next year's student body and revenue.

For individual applicants with different profiles (for example, different academic quality indicators, geographical origin, and financial need), sensitivity curves were developed for estimating students' warmth toward varying levels of financial aid in the form of grants and scholarships. As grants and scholarships increased, loans as a part of the package decreased correspondingly and the probability of enrollment increased. Taking groups of admitted applicants who were homogeneous with respect to academic quality and financial need, the data-mining study also obtained additional sensitivity curves. This information was used to advise and assist the enrollment management staff in making more informed distributions of financial aid.

The enrollment management staff had been using a matrix of academic quality and financial need for admitted applicants to assign amounts of institutional scholarships and proportions of need covered by grant aid. Recom-

NEW DIRECTIONS FOR INSTITUTIONAL RESEARCH • DOI: 10.1002/ir

mendations were then used to modify scholarship amounts and grant proportions within each cell of the matrix.

The data-mining process developed in-house, therefore, was built on existing models rather than abandoning familiar methods historically used by the Admissions Office (that is, the academic-quality-times-financial-need matrix). Financial aid data could now be modified for groups of homogeneous applicants within each cell of the matrix and the resulting expected yields displayed.

Results for the 2004 Class

The managerial results displayed in Table 5.1 were impressive, especially when compared with those obtained in the previous two years by the external consultant. Row one in the table illustrates the percentage variance between the targeted enrollment and the actual enrollment. As can be seen, in the previous years the actual enrollment was more than 15 percent over or under desired enrollment. In 2004, using the model and tools developed in-house, the variance was only 2.5 percent. In terms of variance from the target discount rate using the consultant, the discount rate was between 2 and 3.5 percent off the target. With the in-house model, the variance was less than 1 percent. These results were achieved without losing any academic quality (as indicated by scores on the Scholastic Assessment Test). However, there was a drop in ethnic diversity, which can be emphasized in future model modification efforts.

The model developed in-house was the same type of logistic regression model developed by the consultant. The consultant claimed that its model predicted individuals correctly approximately 70 percent of the time. The data-mining model showed similar results. However, the consultant did not provide individual student- or group-level projections on a timely basis. Thus, the Institutional Research Office did not have the data necessary to provide regular updates or proprietary what-if (decision support) scenarios on demand that allowed the Admissions Office to immediately tailor its financial aid allocations. In summary, the improvements were not primarily because the model provided was better but because the model was more transparent and provided model deployment

Table 5.1. Enrollment Outcomes for New Freshmen

Outcome	2002	2003	2004
Enrollment variance (actual − target) ÷ target (%)	−16.9	+21.1	+2.5
Tuition discount variance (actual − target) ÷ target (%)	−3.5	+2.0	−0.5
SAT median score	1230	1250	1260
Ethnic Minority representation (%)	20.8	19.2	15.4

for real-time and customized application by the institution's internal enrollment management staff.

Conclusion and Future Enhancements

The partnering of faculty, students, and administrators has resulted in improved enrollment management practices. The university is more able to stabilize enrollment and the revenue stream through a combination of statistical modeling and a tool to make the application more user friendly. What-if scenarios are quickly applied to help find the best mix of students and revenue. To wit, this institution has been able to meet new student enrollment goals while increasing the academic quality and its net revenue.

Although the current model is useful, all members of the team agreed that it could be improved by better estimating actual price elasticity for various groups of students. It was also recognized that the deployment model for global results could be generated within the Clementine application. The results can be utilized by institutional research and enrollment management personnel, therefore reducing their workload. These enhancements are planned for future development of this project.

Institutions considering this approach must ask themselves several questions. First, does the institution have the level of expertise necessary to develop precise models? Typically, a graduate program in statistics or management will provide the knowledge base and human resources necessary to develop the models. Schools that do not have these kinds of assets may wish to investigate whether there are other programs at noncompeting institutions that they can leverage. As noted above, the key benefit of the approach is its timeliness and transparency and the user-friendly tools derived. Schools looking outside their own institutions must be sure that they can achieve similar timeliness and transparency from the institution providing the service.

Second, because the MBA students do not have experience in dealing with Admissions Office issues, a school may not want to expect the initial models to be immediately actionable. That is, the models developed in the customized approach must be tested before being used for yield management. The question to ask is "how soon are these estimates needed?" In addition, because of the inexperience of the students, the initial part of the program required significant time and effort from the university personnel. Do the admissions and the institutional research offices have the resources required to engage in these interactions? On the other hand, once the program is on its feet, the resources needed are likely to be much less than those required by hiring an outside consultant.

In summary, small schools with limited staff have typically faced a difficult choice. Do they outsource the enrollment management process, thereby losing control of their most important source of revenue, or do they invest in the personnel to bring the process in-house? This case study illustrates a middle path: to creatively locate institutional resources on campus that can be used without adding professional staff. Schools making this choice should recognize that the start-up costs in time invested by institutional research and admissions personnel are substantial, but such a solution has the potential to provide significant long-term added value to the school.

References

Bontrager, B. "Strategic Enrollment Management: Core Strategies and Best Practices." *College and University Journal,* 2004, *79*(4), 9–16.

Chapman, P., and others. CRISP-DM 1.0, CRISP-DM Consortium. Chicago, Ill.: SPSS, 2000.

Galoti, K., and Mark, M. "How Do High School Students Structure an Important Life Decision? A Short-Term Longitudinal Study of the College Decision Making Process." *Research in Higher Education,* 1994, *17,* 589–607.

Groth, R. *Data Mining: Building Competitive Advantage.* Englewood Cliffs, N.J.: Prentice Hall, 2000.

Hossler, D., Schmit, J., and Vesper, N. *Going to College: How Social, Economic, and Educational Factors Influence the Decisions Students Make.* Baltimore: Johns Hopkins University Press, 1999.

CHRISTOPHER M. ANTONS is director of institutional research and planning support at Willamette University.

ELLIOT N. MALTZ is professor of marketing at Atkinson Graduate School of Management at Willamette University.

6

This chapter explores how multiple approaches including data mining can help examine how the lengths of student enrollment are associated with varying numbers of advanced placement units.

Using Data Mining to Explore Which Students Use Advanced Placement to Reduce Time to Degree

Paul W. Eykamp

Understanding behaviors of continuing students, especially the intensity of their course-taking pattern and the total number of courses they take, is a key aspect of enrollment management. One thing that may affect these behaviors is the advanced placement (AP) units students bring on enrollment. AP units are granted by a university to its enrolled students on the basis of exams administered by the Educational Testing Service. The exams test subject matters learned in high school, and scores of 3, 4, or 5 are awarded, equivalent to grades C, B, or A, in an introductory college course on the subject.

At the University of California System (UC), students have their scores transferred in automatically as part of the admissions process. Credits (but not grades) are automatically awarded for test scores of 3 or higher. It is up to individual campuses, schools, and departments to determine if particular classes can be substituted with AP credits or if such AP credits are nonspecific units that can be counted toward meeting the minimum number of units required for graduation. Some departments and programs do not allow the use of AP units to substitute for introductory courses in a student's major because college introductory courses often contain specific subject matters that may or may not have been covered in high school classes.

The conventional wisdom expects that the number of AP units may be a predictive factor to how long students will stay at an institution and the

NEW DIRECTIONS FOR INSTITUTIONAL RESEARCH, no. 131, Fall 2006 © Wiley Periodicals, Inc.
Published online in Wiley InterScience (www.interscience.wiley.com) • DOI: 10.1002/ir.189

course load they will take. At a minimum, AP units should be able to reduce the total number of university units required for graduation.

Without seeing any data, policymakers (both at UC and in the California state legislature) postulated that students arriving with lots of AP units would be using them to graduate earlier and ruminated out loud about making plans based on this assumption. My cursory examination of the data, however, showed little evidence of a close relationship between AP units and the time to degree. College students in UC are a heterogeneous group. As a result, the connection between AP units and time to degree may not be the same for all students. Therefore, it is more appropriate to understand AP units' effect on students' pace toward degrees within subgroups. If AP use was restricted to a specific group of students, this might affect policy choices as well as the ongoing discussion on the weight assigned to AP classes in the admission process. In other words, if students were not consistently using their AP units, then this would affect projections of continuing student enrollment because rising AP units would not be expected to have a substantial effect on time-to-degree reduction. Apparently there is an urgent need to analyze continuing student enrollment behaviors to inform policy before it moves too far down the decision-making pipeline.

This study examines a cohort of UC students to see what effect AP units have on time to degree, course load, and propensity to double a student's major. The study examines the number of AP units that students had at matriculation to test the assumption that as students accumulate more AP units (which is a strong recent trend), there would be a direct and linear reduction in the number of courses that they would take at the institution. Well over half of the UC students have AP units accepted by the university by virtue of a score of 3 or higher on the AP exam, and many of them have the unit equivalent of an academic quarter or more. Some even have close to a year's worth of units when they matriculate. Yet, despite the rapid growth in AP units, there has not been a corresponding rapid reduction in time-to-degree completion.

Anecdotal evidence indicates that many students use AP scores to place themselves above introductory courses and to start at a more advanced level. This may not speed up their time to degree but, rather, give them a better university experience and increase the total knowledge they acquire by allowing them to take a larger number of advanced courses or to take courses in more subject areas than they would otherwise be able to do in the absence of AP units. This is an important use of the AP exam; indeed, this was the original purpose of the AP exam (College Board, 2006).

Advanced-placement units can also be used to lighten loads, allowing students to do more research or drop a class that turns out to be a poor match without incurring an increased time to degree. With a sizable number of AP units, students may have extra time to work for pay to help defray college expenses. Furthermore, AP units can be used to support double majors that require more units than many students can take in a four-year period, especially if they have to work or have other commitments. Alternatively, because taking AP classes is considered a positive factor in being admitted to a UC institution, AP unit accumulation may simply be seen by students as a means of gaining admission to highly completive campuses and programs. After enrollment, they find that the units are either not useful or prefer to take the normal sequence and number of courses rather than use their AP credits. This was an important area of discussion during the planning process for UC Merced (University of California Office of the President, 2000).

This study was conducted at the system level. Data were aggregated from the eight undergraduate campuses. On careful examination by the author, such data allowed the study of the relationship between the number of AP and other university units brought in by students at matriculation and students' time to degree, the average number of units taken per term, and other general measures of student activity. A caveat of the limitation of aggregate data is discussed at the end of this chapter.

Cohort Description

This study illustrates a data-mining approach to determining how, if at all, students are using the AP and other college units that they bring with them when they enter the UC system. It does not analyze why students do what they do or describe individual paths. The goal of this study is to provide policymakers with basic guidance as to the likely effects of changes in broad policy toward AP units, such as changing the minimum test score required to grant credit or the predictive effect of changes in the number of AP credits earned by students over time on continuing student enrollment and course-taking patterns. To accomplish this, data-mining techniques are used to look at the behavior of all students to find the actual patterns of behavior.

The 1994 cohort of entering first-time freshmen is tracked for six years after they entered. Almost all UC students attend full-time, and most are more or less continuously enrolled. There were 15,667 students in the cohort, who were enrolled an average of thirteen quarters. Assuming a norm of twelve quarters or four years, 9.5 percent graduated early (less than twelve quarters), and 40 percent graduated on time (twelve enrolled quarters or four years). Of those taking longer, 16 percent graduated in thirteen quarters, and a total of about 43 percent take some or all of a fifth year. The students were distributed among eight general campuses, all of which are Carnegie Doctoral or Research Extensive institutions. (UC-Berkeley, which is on a semester system, was converted to quarters by multiplying semester units by 1.5.)

Three-fifths (60 percent) of the incoming freshmen had AP or other university credit when they matriculated. A convenient way of thinking about the amount of AP credit is to convert it into class equivalents, as shown in Table 6.1 (where four AP units equal one class, except at UC-Santa Cruz where the conversion is five units per class). A normal course load is between three and four courses per quarter (three is the minimum

Table 6.1. AP Credit Converted to Class Equivalents

Class Equivalents (no.)	Students (no.)	Percentage
None	6,229	39.76
<1 full class[a]	2,248	14.34
1–2	1,724	11.00
3–4	2,284	14.58
5–7	872	5.57
8–12	807	5.15
13–16+	193	1.23

[a]Classes can be three or four units, and some students seem to have been given three units.

for acceptable progress and four the more normal load). Seminars and laboratory classes carry other unit values but typically cannot be replaced by AP units.

Many students have a small amount of AP credit, with 25 percent of those with units having two or fewer course equivalents. On the other hand, some 4,000 students have enough units to potentially replace a quarter's worth of work or more.

Regression Analysis

One feature of data mining is that it is possible to "go fishing" in a large data set for patterns that might explain behaviors. With small data sets, it is typically required that one start with a hypothesis, and statistical procedures are used to demonstrate that the hypothesized outcome is different from what might occur from random chances. A small number of observations means that the relationship must be reasonably strong to show statistical significance.

With the large data sets used in data mining, statistical significance is generally not the problem (see Chapter One for a more detailed explanation). It is important to have a reasonable expectation that a relationship is meaningful—that users can act on the knowledge that the relationship exists and the magnitude is large enough to make a difference. Of course, what constitutes "meaningful" depends on the context and the question being asked.

In this case, we have an input (AP units) and specific outcomes (time to degree, total number of units earned). We do not know if they are related or if any other variables (such as family income) may influence the relationship.

Often data mining involves esoteric data analysis techniques, but it is useful and important for this case study to first start with the simple hypothesis and easily understood techniques so that readers can have a common point of reference.

The first analysis attempted was to run a simple linear regression analysis of a cohort of students to see if there was any predictive value in the number of AP units on time to degree. It seemed plausible that if many students were using their AP credit to replace UC credits, a larger number of AP units should be clearly associated with shorter degree times.

HYPOTHESIS: *Number of AP units taken should be strongly and negatively correlated with time to degree.*

The first regression runs were disappointing in this regard. A simple regression of the number of AP or other units at matriculation against the total enrolled quarters yielded a parameter estimate in the right direction but with a small magnitude: one-third of a quarter expected reduction in time to degree per a quarter's worth of AP units. However, the adjusted R^2 was only 0.0349. The intercept was also one-third of a quarter larger than the dependent mean. This means that whereas for the UC system there was some correlation between AP units and time to degree and the tendency was in the hoped-for direction, there was almost no predictive value in terms of more units leading consistently to a shorter time to degree; instead, there was a steep discount on the value of AP units.

It is possible that a better predictive value would be found in smaller groups of students who shared some characteristic and who were being swamped by the general population. For example, patterns may exist for groups of students with majors such as engineering and physical sciences (who are generally more constrained in how AP units can be used). One way of looking for patterns simply was to run regressions separately for humanities, social science, science, or engineering students. Each campus was analyzed separately, and students with at least four AP units were separated out. To test the idea that students with stronger records behave differently from those with weaker records, a regression model that used both the number of AP units and the students' academic index ([(high school grade-point average [GPA] × 1,000) + SAT I + SAT II, where SAT refers to Scholastic Assessment Test], which is a standard UC uses to control for student quality) to predict time to degree.

In case the relationship was not linear at the extremes, the model was also run for a variety of subgroups toward the middle of the distribution (that is, between four and twenty-four AP units, eight and twenty-four, eight and thirty-four, and so on) Alternatively, nonlinear regression techniques could have been used, possibly more effectively, but these are harder to explain to policymakers, so the simpler approach was tried first. For a discussion of non-linear regression and other techniques to properly analyze non-normal data, see "Introduction to Regression" (Princeton, 2006).

For most permutations of the type of student (science versus nonscience) or AP unit count, the coefficients stayed in the range of 0.02 to 0.05 quarters per unit, and the R^2 hovered between 0.03 and 0.09. The higher values were found for science, math, or engineering students with at least four AP units. Average time to degree was slightly lower (about 0.1 quarter) for students with at least four AP units, which is the number needed to replace a class. Anecdote has it that a fair number of students find themselves about four units (one class) short of the 180-quarter units needed to graduate at the end of their fourth year, and four AP units may come to the rescue at that point, though in many cases that may affect only summer school attendance. This would not affect the time to degree because summer is not counted.

The slightly higher value for science students was somewhat unexpected because typically these students have the most restrictions on the use of AP credit to replace courses. It was expected that they would have the lowest parameter estimate and a lower R^2, but the opposite was true. Possibly the correlation was higher because science and engineering students have more structured programs, which make their use of AP units more consistent. In any case, the R^2 was small, and there was little predictive power available.

The first hypothesis failed for the entire cohort, except for a weak negative correlation between the number of AP units and the time to degree. It is not possible to draw systemwide conclusions from regression analysis about the effect of changes in number of AP units on students' time to degree, except in the loosest possible terms. Clearly AP units were having some effect in reducing time to degree, but there was a lot of noise overwhelming whatever signal was contained in the data. Even for students graduating in four years or less, there was not much predictive power in the number of AP units brought in. Apparently summer school and other factors outweighed AP units for influencing faster completion times.

On a campus-by-campus basis, the story was much the same, with a low R^2 and small negative parameter estimates. An exception was at UC-Riverside, which had a much stronger correlation. UC-Riverside's regression model produced an adjusted R^2 of 0.19 for all students and 0.24 for students with at least four AP units. The parameter estimate was higher as well, with 0.05 fewer quarters per AP unit estimated (0.75 quarters per quarter of AP units). In addition to a stronger R^2 was the significant difference in the average number of enrolled quarters between all students and those with at least four AP units: 12.7 quarters for all students and 12.3 for students with at least four AP units. This was a much greater difference than was seen for a similar division either systemwide or at other individual campuses.

For some reason, UC-Riverside students alone in the system can be predicted as a group to use their AP and other college credits brought in at matriculation to reduce their time to degree and are much more efficient at converting AP units into reduced time to degree. There is no immediate obvious difference in UC-Riverside students that might explain this. Like the system as a whole, UC-Riverside had a large fraction of students with at least four AP units, about 53 percent (versus 56 percent for the system). It also has a similar fraction of science and engineering students.

NEW DIRECTIONS FOR INSTITUTIONAL RESEARCH • DOI: 10.1002/ir

One theory was that lower-income students (who are somewhat predominant at UC-Riverside) might have a higher propensity to use their AP units. However, when parental income was added to the regression equation for the system as a whole, the R^2 remained low. Additional research is needed to determine what is different at UC-Riverside and if there is a finding that can be generalized.

From an enrollment management perspective, at this one campus a simple regression analysis provides evidence that the number of AP units could generally help predict the time to degree. Multiyear-trend analysis is needed to specify what the prediction should be and how it changes over time.

For the system (and the rest of the campuses), there was no clear regression model with strong predictive power, and because anecdotal evidence indicates that a significant number of students were using AP units, a different analytical approach was needed.

Decision Tree Analysis

Because the more traditional statistical methods did not produce any significant results (except for one campus), alternative methods were considered. The study started with the method that was easiest to explain to policymakers (and outside audiences). That method is decision tree analysis, which splits observations by the breaks that lead to clusters of outcomes in a way that can be explained in plain English, such as "students with more than x units had this outcome on average whereas students with fewer than x tended to have another outcome."

Using this tool, it was possible to look for breaking points and find the point at which AP units were associated with a reduced time to degree. Students with more than 13 AP units had a shorter time to degree than those who had fewer than 13 units, and those with more than 27.75 had about half a quarter less time enrolled than average for all students with AP units. A small number of students who had more than 74 units of AP graduated quickly as is shown by the students in the white box in Figure 6.1.

This analysis confirmed the results of the regression model and provided a better way of finding the points at which having a certain number of AP units affected the number of quarters enrolled. It further illustrated that having a lot of AP units, almost two quarters worth, netted an average reduction in time enrolled of only half a term. A small group of students ($n = 18$) who had a large number of AP units (at least 74.7) did graduate much faster than other students, as might be expected.

It is possible to use more than two "leaves" per cycle to break up groups into smaller units and perhaps find smaller pockets where students exhibit similar behavior. Using a four-leafed tree, it could more clearly be seen that linear reductions occurred in time to degree as AP units went up, but the rate of reduction of time enrolled was uniformly slow in comparison with the

Figure 6.1. Decision Tree for Time to Degree

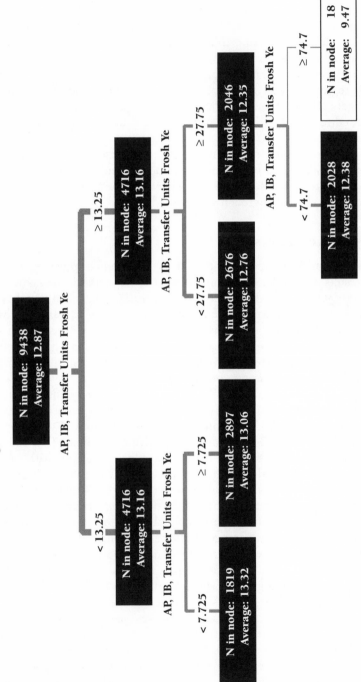

Note: IB = international baccalaureate, Frosh Ye = freshman year (units transferred in during freshman year). This figure illustrates a two-leafed decision tree.

number of AP units. Time enrolled did not fall below four years until the 51-unit point was reached (3.4 quarters' worth of units).

The decision tree method illustrated a mild effect of increased AP units on time to degree. It showed the specific cases (the eighteen students who graduated quickly) that perhaps are the source of some of the anecdotal data (Figure 6.2).

Additional analysis of parental income, academic index, high-unit majors, average course load, and double majors failed to yield any identifiable subgroups that deviated from the general trend; in other words, a large number of AP units yielded small reductions in the number of quarters enrolled. Attributes one would expect to increase the time to degree (lower income, double majors, lower average units enrolled per term, and so forth) had the same effect on all levels of AP unit completion. This seems to indicate (again) that students who have a large number of AP units may (or may not) use them to reduce their time to degree but do not do so in a consistent manner.

This set of results was surprising because it deviates from nearly all the accepted wisdom of how students view their AP units and the desire to graduate early whenever an easy opportunity (such as already achieved units) presents itself. However, this analysis illustrates the value of data mining in disproving a series of widely accepted conventional wisdom "facts."

Other Data-Mining Approaches

Because the decision tree analysis was unsuccessful, a number of additional statistical methods were tried such as cluster analysis, factor analysis, and neural network analysis. Cluster analysis has similar attributes to decision tree analysis in that each decision tree intersection is essentially a division of a sample into two separate groups. However, it is less path dependent because it looks for clusters without regard to previous branching. But cluster analysis also failed to identify distinct groups.

There was still some hope that factor analysis, which looks at several variables at the same time, might detect some synergistic relationships when several variables were all present at the same level. However, nothing came to light. This again is useful in dispelling erroneous conventional wisdom.

Neural network analysis is more or less the ultimate black box in data mining because the results are often hard to explain. Again, in this study, no apparently meaningful interactions were found. Thus, none of the common data-mining techniques yielded any useful predictive insights based on the number of AP units nor did any other attributes produce any homogeneous subgroups.

Subgroup Behavior

If the overly broad group may be masking individual student behaviors, perhaps there were identifiable subgroups among whom having AP units sped

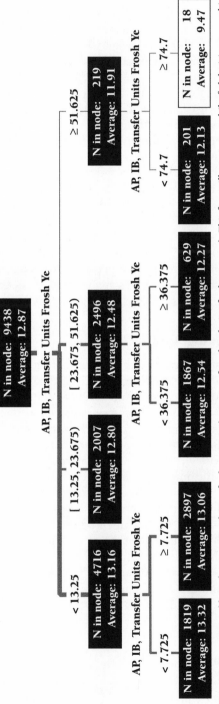

Figure 6.2. Decision Tree for Time to Degree

Note: IB = international baccalaureate, Frosh Ye = freshman year (units transferred in during freshman year). This figure illustrates a multileafed decision tree, which better illustrates the small reduction in average quarters to degree per AP/IB/freshman transfer units.

up time to degree. Because looking forward from the starting point of the initial granting of AP units could not uncover subgroups with distinctive characteristics, they may be identifiable by looking backward from examining attributes of the students who did use their AP units.

This means that it was necessary to identify students who actually used AP units to graduate. Did these students take more or less time than average to complete their degree? We know that some students graduated in less than four years with fewer than 180 UC units. So they seemed like potential candidates for AP unit users. Can the study predict who will finish early based on students' specific characteristics? One way to answer this question is to study the average course load taken by students with and without AP units to see if students are substituting AP units for UC units as they proceed. This use of AP units might not have shown up in the other analyses because those centered on time to degree as the dependent variable.

Students Needing Non-UC Units to Graduate. UC degrees require at least 180-quarter units to graduate, and the university's data systems differentiate between UC units and units earned at other institutions. Clearly, students who graduated with fewer than 180 UC-generated units would have had to use either AP units or other units that were transferred in after the freshman year (that is, summer session units or community college or other institutions' units taken over the summer or concurrently).

The data collected in the systemwide database do not record whether AP units were used to fulfill specific requirements; it simply records their presence for fulfilling the minimum number of units. Thus, it is possible that students with 20 AP units and 179 UC units will still not be able to graduate because they are missing a specific course that the AP units do not replace. Because of this, there is a certain amount of guesswork involved in determining exactly which AP units were used. This again is a matter best researched at the campus level. However, it is still possible to generate some approximate values for the role of AP units.

In the 1994 cohort of entering first-time freshmen who graduated, 6,117 (39 percent) needed AP or transfer units earned after their freshman year to bring them up to 180 units. Not all of these students had enough AP units to make up the deficit. Certain student actions toward the end of their undergraduate careers allow us to know with some certainty that they did or did not use AP units.

Summer Degree Students. Some students received their degrees over the summer and needed eight or fewer units. Because the normal summer course load is eight units, it seems reasonable to assume that students getting their degrees over the summer who needed only two classes would not take summer school if their other non-UC units would fulfill the requirements.

Of 2,603 students who got their degrees over the summer, 1,541 needed eight or fewer units, most of whom (1,236) had no AP units. So the assumption that none of them used AP units seems fairly safe. This brings the total number of students not directly using AP units to shorten the time to degree (or at least the 180 units of a UC workload) to 11,090 or 70 percent of the entering cohort who graduated within the six years of the study.

On the other hand, we can be fairly certain that the 1,062 students who needed more than eight units and received summer degrees used some non-UC units. There were also 281 students who did not appear to have enough units from any source to graduate. Presumably some of these were errors caught after the data tapes were submitted to systemwide scrutiny, and some are students who "found" courses that they had taken outside of UC and transferred in at the last minute. This leaves the study with 1,343 students who needed non-UC units (including AP units) of those who graduated over the summer. These students may have used AP units to graduate, and their analysis is described in the next section.

Students with Unit Deficits. After students who got degrees in the summer (removing those who needed only eight units and apparently took them over the summer) were taken into account, there were 3,260 students who needed more non-UC units than they had AP units in order to graduate (Table 6.2). This does not help determine which students used AP units but does illustrate the magnitude of units brought in from outside the regular university program to help meet requirements; moreover, it shows that AP units are not the largest source of non-UC units. For this cohort, UC summer programs are treated like external transfer units.

Moving back to the original question, a matrix of unit deficits and AP units available indicates that there were 2,984 students who could meet all of their unit deficits with AP units. There are no data to indicate whether they actually used AP units (or other units brought in when they matriculated) or if they used other transfer units earned after matriculation. Students may or may not have had the option of using AP units because requirements for specific courses and other limits may have precluded their use.

Table 6.2. Students with Fewer than 180 UC Units Requiring Units Beyond AP Units

Units Required to Graduate Beyond AP	Number of Students	Percentage
1–4	779	23.90
5–8	542	16.63
9–12	840	25.77
13–20	596	18.28
21–28	252	7.73
29–36	123	3.77
>36	128	3.93
Total	3,260	100.00

One way of getting around this problem is to assume that transfer units earned after matriculation would have a greater chance of being used than AP units because presumably the students had a better idea of what courses were needed after they started college than what they may have earned before enrolling. Presumably students would not go to the trouble and expense of getting additional units from an outside institution once they had started at UC unless they had a clear need for them. Therefore, it is assumed that units transferred after the freshman year will be used first to make up the deficit.

Starting with that assumption, the total number of non-AP units earned (in other words, transfer units earned after the freshman year) was subtracted from the non-UC units needed to graduate. The balance represents units that had to be filled from the AP unit stock. If the above assumption is true, then these represent the minimum number of AP units used.

The actual number will be somewhat higher because it is likely that not all transfer units were utilized if an AP unit fit better (or got counted first). In addition, some postfreshman year transfer units may have been taken for interest rather than for need or for a need that never materialized. However, the number of such units should be small.

If we assume that these were the only AP units used to replace UC units and that all other units required came from other postfreshman year sources, we expect that AP units shortened the time to degree by at least one quarter for 2,874 students (18.3 percent of the total number of freshmen in the cohort). An additional 1,335 students (8.5 percent) should have reduced their time to degree by two quarters, and about 279 (1.8 percent) saved three or more quarters. Actual quarters not enrolled depend on the number of units per quarter earned: twelve is approximately the minimum needed to count as making adequate progress. The total number of person-quarters saved would be about 6,161, or 2,054 full-time equivalent. This does not mean that students graduated faster; some of them may simply have taken fewer UC units, reducing the university's workload but not its head count.

Average Course Load

Another way students might make use of AP units is to reduce their course load while they are enrolled—that is, take the normal amount of time to graduate but reduce their average number of courses per term. Table 6.3 illustrates that students who used AP units to graduate had lighter course loads than did students who did not use AP units.

Because a linear regression is the most straightforward (more AP units means fewer courses taken per term), the analysis again started there. And again, the results were significant, in the correct direction, and had a tiny adjusted R^2. This was true for a number of restrictions on the number of AP units (all, middle range, nonzero, and so forth) and on the average number of units taken, for total to date, the last term enrolled, and for restricted sets.

NEW DIRECTIONS FOR INSTITUTIONAL RESEARCH • DOI: 10.1002/ir

Table 6.3. Students Who Needed AP Units to Graduate, Having Exhausted Transfer Units Earned After Freshman Year

AP Units Required to Graduate	Number of Students	Percentage
1–4	969	6.27
5–8	1,206	7.81
9–12	699	4.52
13–20	922	5.97
21–28	413	2.67
29–36	161	1.04
>36	118	0.76
Total needing AP units	4,488	29.05
Total needing no AP units	10,962	70.95
Missing[a]	217	0.95

[a]Students with lost records due to ID number changes.

However, if the average course load for all students is compared with that of students who needed to use AP units to graduate, then a pattern of a lighter course load is clearly observed. It is evident why there is a predictive relationship on an individual student level because plotting the averages seems to generate a clear result (Figure 6.3).

Figure 6.3. Percentage of Graduating Students with Various Course Loads

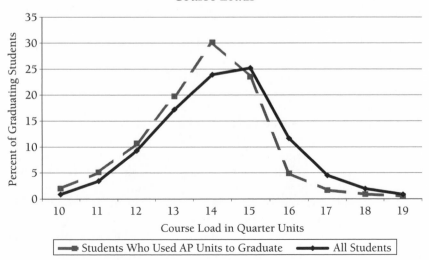

If one looks only at the last year the student was enrolled before earning a degree, it is apparent that there exists a tendency for students who used their AP units to take a slightly lighter load than students in general (Figure 6.4).

Decision tree analysis also failed to identify any additional characteristic determining which students would choose to use their AP units to reduce their course load other than the tautology that some who could did in fact reduce their average load.

High-Unit Majors and Double Majors

Another belief commonly held was that students who take majors that have a large number of requirements, leading to more than 180-quarter units required for graduation, or students taking double majors will tend to be the students with the most AP units.

Figure 6.5 shows that the opposite seems to be true. Students with a large number of AP units are slightly less likely to graduate with high-unit or double majors than those graduating with normal 180-quarter-unit majors.

Students without any AP units seemed equally likely to take high-unit or double majors as to major in a field without any special requirements.

Regression analysis failed to show any relationship between AP units and the academic index (see above), which was also an expected relationship. This was true for all students and the subset of students with more than twenty AP units.

Figure 6.4. Average Number of Units Per Term, Final Year

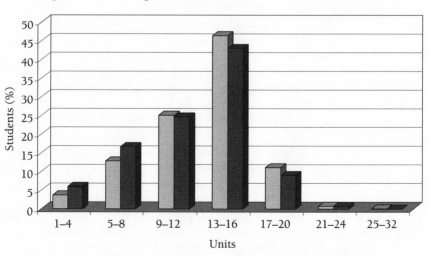

□ All Students   ■ Students who used AP Units to Graduate

NEW DIRECTIONS FOR INSTITUTIONAL RESEARCH • DOI: 10.1002/ir

Figure 6.5. Students in High-Unit and Double Majors by Number of AP Units

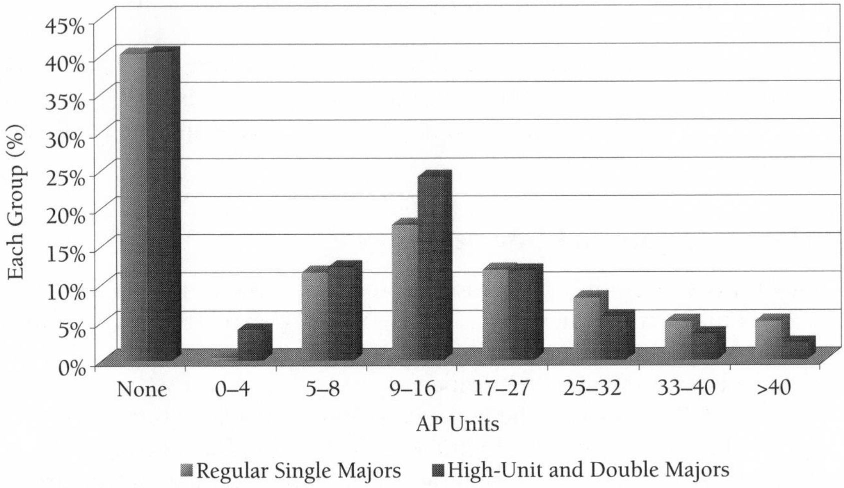

■Regular Single Majors   ■High-Unit and Double Majors

Conclusions

The failure of the regression model to show a clear and strong linear relationship between time to degree and the number of AP and other college units brought into the UC at matriculation indicates that a simple model of straight unit-for-unit replacement may not be sufficient. Some students clearly substitute AP units for UC units, and we can determine with some degree of certainty that about one-third of the entering freshman cohort uses at least a few AP units to substitute for course work they would otherwise have to take at the university. Some students, about 10 percent, substitute more than 1 quarter's worth of courses. It is also clear that about 70 percent of students do not need the AP units (if any) because they earn 180 or more UC units. Because double majors and certain high-unit majors require more than 180 units, these figures are not exact, and the number of students requiring AP and transfer units to graduate is understated.

Decision tree analysis shows that students with a large number of AP units (more than twenty-seven) tend to enroll for slightly fewer quarters than those with fewer AP units, but the two quarters' worth of units is associated with only half a quarter less time enrolled, an average that still exceeds four years. Only about two hundred students with vast numbers of AP units (more than fifty-one) form a coherent group that beats the four-year mark. Although it appears that AP units have a linear relationship with a reduced time to degree from decision tree analysis, the relationship is clearly weak, and a large number of students at each range of AP units held by the students do not appear to use their AP units to reduce their time to degree.

NEW DIRECTIONS FOR INSTITUTIONAL RESEARCH • DOI: 10.1002/ir

Although AP units present no apparent predictable effect on the average number of units taken per term, they bear some association with the total number of student quarters enrolled and total courses taken per student term. Students who earn fewer than 180 UC units and need their AP units to graduate take fewer units per term than the overall cohort.

From this we can infer that about a third of UC students make use of their AP units to graduate, and many of them take a slightly lighter course load as a way of using their AP units. At this level of analysis, we cannot predict which individual students will use their AP units or how they will use them if they choose to do so. In fact, it appears that the factors influencing student use of AP units are nearly entirely exogenous.

Additional transcript-level analysis at the campus level may provide better answers about the conditions under which students decide to use AP units and other transfer credits they brought with them as incoming freshmen. The systemwide data do not provide clear answers other than to show that, in aggregate, AP units do matter but not in a way that can be predicted for individual students a priori.

References

College Board. "The History of the AP Program: A Half-Century of Excellence in American Education." 2006. http://apcentral.collegeboard.com/apc/public/program/history/8019.html. Accessed Jan. 18, 2006.

Princeton University Data and Statistical Services. "Introduction to Regression." 2006. http://dss.princeton.edu/online_help/analysis/regression_intro.htm. Accessed Jan. 18, 2006.

University of California Office of the President. "Thinking in Future Tense: Designing the New Architecture of Student Life at UC Merced." Oakland, Calif.: Final report of the UC Merced Student Planning Committee, 2000.

PAUL W. EYKAMP is coordinator of long-range enrollment analysis and database development for academic and strategic planning and analysis at the University of California Office of the President in Oakland, California.

NEW DIRECTIONS FOR INSTITUTIONAL RESEARCH • DOI: 10.1002/ir

7

Data mining of IPEDS data is used to develop models that calculate predicted graduation rates for two- and four-year institutions.

Let the Data Talk: Developing Models to Explain IPEDS Graduation Rates

Brenda L. Bailey

Institutional researchers are often called on to work with graduation rates. All postsecondary education institutions participating in Title IV are required by the Student Right-to-Know Act to make available reports containing their graduation rate (National Center for Education Statistics, 2000). The National Center for Education Statistics collects graduation rate data with the Integrated Postsecondary Education Data System (IPEDS) Graduation Rate Survey (GRS). An institution's graduation rate has extensive influence on its policies and practices, accountability, and assessment.

Astin (1993) argued that reporting graduation rates without reporting supplementary information should be questioned. Astin recommends that both the actual and predicted rates provide useful information. Student Right-to-Know disclosure forms can be made more meaningful with the addition of predicted graduation rates. An institution's predicted graduation rate provides additional meaningful information and lends itself readily to the practice of benchmarking for identifying comparable peer groups or segments of institutions in order to understand graduation rates in meaningful and appropriate contexts.

The IPEDS is a multidimensional and complex data system, naturally a rich place for conducting a variety of data mining. With any kind of databases that contain multidimensional subjects and span multiple years, data mining is an ideal approach to identify hidden patterns and discover future trends or behaviors. Luan (2002) noted that "data mining is the process of discovering hidden messages, patterns, and knowledge within

large amounts of data and making predictions for outcomes or behaviors" (p. 17). It is a tool that can find patterns in a database as complex as IPEDS and produce predicted graduation rates based on those patterns. The purpose of this study was to employ data-mining techniques to develop models that calculate predicted graduation rates at both two-year and four-year institutions in the Minnesota state system. The results can provide institutions with contextual information to assist in the interpretation of graduation rates reported to Student Right-to-Know.

Integrated Postsecondary Education Data System

The 2000 redesign of IPEDS included the development of the IPEDS Peer Analysis System, a higher education data-search tool that makes national IPEDS data available to researchers in a timely manner. The IPEDS collection includes data about institutional characteristics, completions, human resources, enrollment, finance, student financial aid, and graduation rates. The IPEDS Peer Analysis System "provides a more readily accessible and comprehensive approach to accessing institutional data for benchmarking with appropriate institutional peer groups than other methods of data collection" (Schuh, 2002, p. 29).

IPEDS is a complex, comprehensive federal database with enormous amounts of data about all higher education institutions. The data dictionary downloaded from the IPEDS Peer Analysis System lists over a thousand variables. IPEDS data from 1980 through 2004 are currently available. The GRS added to IPEDS data collection in 1997 enables the consistent collection of graduation rate data using standard definitions.

Data Source

The population for this study was all postsecondary institutions responding to the GRS in 2003. Table 7.1 shows a count by control and level of these 5,771 institutions.

The 2003 GRS includes graduation rate data for cohort year 1997 for four-year institutions and cohort year 2000 for two-year and less institutions. It collects data for cohorts of full-time, first-time, and degree- or certificate-seeking students by race and gender. In addition to the GRS, other data were also downloaded, including the 2003 Institutional Characteristics, Fall Enrollment, Postsecondary Completions, Faculty Salaries, Fall Staff, Employees by Assigned Position, Finance, and Student Financial Aid surveys. Also downloaded were frequently used and derived IPEDS variables used in the IPEDS Data Feedback Report. This report was developed by the National Postsecondary Education Cooperative to provide a context for examining IPEDS data (National Postsecondary Education Cooperative, 2004).

**Table 7.1. Distribution of Institutions
by Control and Level**

Control and Level	Count
Public, two-year and less	1,421
Public, four-year	586
Private, not-for-profit, less than two-year	114
Private, not-for-profit, two-year only	221
Private, not-for-profit, four-year	1,273
Private, for-profit, less than two-year	1,223
Private, for-profit, two-year only	722
Private, for-profit, four-year	211
Total	5,771

In this type of large-scale analysis involving a complex data system, "understanding the database in which data reside and the data characteristics (structured and unstructured) [is] essential to successful data mining" (Luan, 2002, p. 27). IPEDS data are summary data at the institutional level, not at the student unit record level. The Peer Analysis System includes multiple files for some IPEDS surveys and single files for others. Some files include a single row of data for each institution, and others contain multiple rows of data for each institution. For example, the Institutional Characteristics Survey is segmented into four files, each containing one row of data for the institution. One file contains directory information such as the Carnegie classification code, control, and level of the institution. A second file contains educational offerings, accreditation, admissions, services, and athletic associations. The third file contains student charges for academic year programs, and the fourth file contains student charges by program. The Completions Survey is found in only one file, but the data are segmented within this one file into multiple rows of data for each institution by a six-digit Classification of Instructional Programs (CIP) code, award level, race, and gender. There are six Enrollment Survey files, two Faculty Salaries Survey files, four Fall Staff Survey files, one Employees by Assigned Position file, six Finance Survey files, one Student Financial Survey file, and three GRS files.

After an understanding of the IPEDS database and data characteristics was acquired, the next step was to download the IPEDS data from the Peer Analysis System using the Dataset Cutting Tool. Data were downloaded into Microsoft Excel Comma Separated Values files and imported into Microsoft Access. Access and SPSS software were used to build the data-mining files. The actual data mining was done with Clementine 9.0 software. It was easy for the researcher to move the data between Access, SPSS, and Clementine. The researcher was most familiar with Microsoft Access, and the data-mining files were therefore built with Access queries. The researcher was less familiar with Clementine and reserved this software for the actual data-mining steps. One limitation to this method was the number of variables allowed in an Access table. The IPEDS data downloaded for this project included over a thousand variables. A single row of data that contained these one thousand variables was built for each institution. This was accomplished with eighty Access queries that created six data-mining files. These six files were imported into SPSS and merged together as one data-mining file. This SPSS data file served as the data source for data mining with Clementine.

Data-Mining Model Development

Major data-mining applications manage the entire data analysis process as a data stream with the data flowing from the original source all the way to the last procedure, typically a clustering algorithm or a predictive algorithm. An algorithm is a procedure for conducting specific tasks and is visually represented by a node. Figure 7.1 shows the Clementine data stream used in the analysis. A separate data stream with the same nodes was developed for each model. The sequence of operations shown in this visual interface in

Figure 7.1. Depiction of Public Four-Year Data Stream

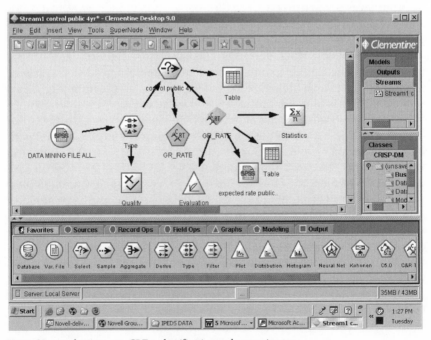

Note: GR = graduation rate, CRT = classification and regression tree.

Clementine is known as a "data stream" because the data flow from the source through each operation in the stream to the destination, which can be a model or some type of data output.

The algorithm selected for the analysis was the classification and regression tree (C&RT). C&RT is a tree-based method of classification and prediction with binary splits. C&RT models are robust in the presence of missing data and a large number of fields. In addition, C&RT models tend to be easier to understand. This tree method is particularly well suited to data mining and revealing simple relationships between variables that could be overlooked using other methods (StatSoft, Inc., 1984). This algorithm "builds classification and regression trees for predicting continuous dependent variables (regression) and categorical predictor variables (classification)" (StatSoft, Inc., 1984). An advantage of this algorithm is that "the dependent variable and predictor variables can be nominal or ordinal (categorical) or interval (scale)" (The Measurement Group, 1999). It is an ideal tool for producing predicted graduation rates using the large number of variables (referred to as "fields" in data mining) available in IPEDS data.

The first data stream to be run included the entire population of 5,771 institutions. The software examined input fields and split records into segments with similar output field values. The graduation rate was set as the output variable, and all other IPEDS variables were set as input fields. Based on predictor input field values, institutions were subjectively segmented into comparison groups by the researcher, and these groups are called *peer groups* in this study. The predicted graduation rate is the average graduation rate for each peer group. The researcher also calculated the weighted predicted rate for each peer group.

Model Specification

Over one thousand IPEDS variables were included as input to the analysis. Of these, Clementine chose fifty-one input variables as predictor variables to place institutions into peer groups based on the graduation rate output variable. Table 7.2 shows the source of these fifty-one predictor variables. Most of the variables came from the Enrollment and Institutional Characteristics surveys. At one each, the Staff, Finance, and Completions surveys contributed the fewest number of predictor variables. Most of the variables in a model are unique to that particular model. Only four predictor variables appear in more than one model. These four repeating predictor variables are adjusted cohort, total completers within 150 percent of normal time, full-year-undergraduate white enrollment, and state affiliation.

Twenty-one models were developed for examination. The models were primarily based on the traditional institutional control as prescribed by the Carnegie classifications. There were eight models for public institutions and thirteen for private institutions. Each model contains key predictive variables to describe the estimated graduation rate. Tables 7.3 through 7.5 show

Table 7.2. Source of Predictor Variables

Survey	Count
Enrollment	22
Institutional Characteristics	19
Student Financial Aid	2
Graduation Rate	2
Salaries	2
NPEC-Salaries	1
Staff	1
NPEC-Finance	1
Completions	1
Total	51

Table 7.3. Models and Predictors for Public Institutions

Model	Predictor

Model 3: Public Two-Year and Less

Adjusted cohort
Enrollment age, 18-19 years, women
Enrollment age, 20-21 years, women
Enrollment age, 22-24 years, men

First Split: Highest degree offered

Total completers within 150 percent of normal time

Model 2: Public Four-Year

Average faculty salary, male
Average faculty salary, professor, male
Enrollment, American Indian
First-time, degree-seeking, enrolled part-time, men
Full-time enrollment, women
Full-time retention rate
Full-year unduplicated head count, women
Percentage of scholarship expenditures from Pell grants
Percentage of first-time degree-seeking students submitting SAT scores

First Split: Percentage of full-time enrollment that is white

Percentage receiving institutional grant aid
SAT 1 Math 75th percentile score
State of institution
Total completers within 150 percent of normal time
Total dormitory capacity

Note: SAT = Scholastic Assessment Test.

NEW DIRECTIONS FOR INSTITUTIONAL RESEARCH • DOI: 10.1002/ir

Table 7.4. Models and Predictors for Private For-Profit Institutions

Model	Predictor

Model 8: Private, For-Profit, Less than Two-Year
> Adjusted cohort

First Split: Total completers within 150 percent of normal time

Model 7: Private, For-Profit, Two-Year Only
> Adjusted cohort
> Full-year undergraduate total enrollment
> State abbreviation code of institution

First Split: Total completed within 150 percent of normal time

Model 1: Private, For-Profit, Four-Year
> Carnegie Classification code
> Enrollment age, 20-21 years, total
> First-time, degree-seeking, enrolled part-time, women
> Full-year, unduplicated graduate head count, nonresident alien
> Full-year, unduplicated undergraduate head count, Hispanic
> Percentage of enrollment that is first-time
> Percentage of enrollment that is first-time, men

First Split: Percentage of enrollment that is men
> Service or maintenance staff, men
> State of institution
> State of residence when student was first admitted
> Total awards: computer and information sciences
> Total completers within 150 percent of normal time
> Tuition plan, restricted

the predictor variables for each of the first seven models of public institutions. The variables are listed in alphabetical order, with the first split highlighted. The model for public four-year institutions contains the most predictor variables. About half of these predictors are related to race or gender, such as salaries for male faculty and enrollment by race or gender. Most of the predictors are related to student characteristics. This is consistent with Astin's (1993) research showing that graduation rates are more about who attends an institution than what the institution actually does for students. This is more apparent with the model containing public two-year and less institutions, in which predictors are all student related. This model contains the most predictors based on the age by gender of the students.

To get a sense of the importance of the predictor variables, it is helpful to view a model tree. C&RT is a tree-based classification and prediction method with binary splits. Institutions are placed in peer groups based on values at each binary split. The predictor variables differ not just by model but also along branches of a particular model. For example, Figure 7.2

NEW DIRECTIONS FOR INSTITUTIONAL RESEARCH • DOI: 10.1002/ir

Table 7.5. Models and Predictors for Private Not-for-Profit Institutions

Model	Predictor
Model 4: Private, Not-for-Profit, Less than Two-Year	
	Books and supplies in largest program
	CIP code of largest program
	Degree of urbanization
	Full-year undergraduate, white enrollment
	Full-time black enrollment
First Split: Regional accrediting agency	
	Offers programs not leading to a formal award
	State of institution
	Total completers within 150 percent of normal time
Model 5: Private, Not-for-Profit Two-Year Only	
First Split: 12-month instructional activity credit hours: undergraduates	
	Average amount of institutional grant aid received
	Calendar system
	Current-year GRS cohort as a percentage of entering class
	Full-year undergraduate, white enrollment
	None of the special learning opportunities are offered
	Off campus, not with family, other expenses
	Off campus, with family, other expenses
	Percentage of full-time enrollment that is men
	Percentage of undergraduate enrollment that is black
	State of institution
	Total completers within 150 percent of normal time

Note: CIP = Classification of Instruction Programs.

shows the public two-year and less model tree. The highest branch is the highest degree offered, splitting at no degree (0) or associate degree (40). Figure 7.3 shows the public four-year model tree. Here the first split is at the percentage of full-time enrollment that is white. Institutions with a percentage of 79.2 percent or less form one branch whereas institutions with a percentage greater than 79.2 percent form the second branch. In the tables of model predictors, the first binary split for each model is highlighted.

Model Results

The researcher ran all twenty-one models with various combinations of control and level. The twenty-one models were assigned model numbers based on the correlation between the actual graduation rate and the predicted graduation rate. Model 1 has the highest correlation, and Model 21 has the lowest correlation.

Figure 7.2. Public Two-Year and Less Model Tree

Hdegoffr in ["0"] [Mode: 9]
   Completers ≤ 4.500 [Mode: 0] ≥ 0.446
   Completers > 4.500 [Mode: 9]
      A2224m ≤ 17.500 [Mode: 9]
         COHORT ≤ 45.500 [Mode: 9] ≥ 0.826
         COHORT > 45.500 [Mode: 8] ≥ 0.732
      A2224m >17.500 [Mode: 9] ≥ 0.632
Hdegoffr in ["40"] [Mode: 1]
   A1819w ≤ 107 [Mode: 4]
      Completers ≤ 17.500 [Mode: 1] ≥ 0.243
      Completers > 17.500 [Mode: 4]
         Completers ≤ 73.500 [Mode: 4]
            COHORT ≤ 52 [Mode: 7] ≥ 0.661
            COHORT > 52 [Mode: 4] ≥ 0.387
         Completers > 73.500 [Mode: 7] ≥ 0.659
   A1819w > 107 [Mode: 1]
      Completers ≤ 88.500 [Mode: 1]
         COHORT ≤ 355 [Mode: 1]
            Completers ≤ 44.500 [Mode: 1] ≥ 0.177
            Completers > 44.500 [Mode: 2] ≥ 0.28
         COHORT > 355 [Mode: 0] ≥ 0.104
      Completers > 88.500 [Mode: 2]
         A2021w ≤ 280.500 [Mode: 3] ≥ 0.403
         A2021w > 280.500 [Mode: 2]
            Completers ≤ 243.500 [Mode: 2] ≥ 0.234
            Completers > 243.500 [Mode: 3] ≥ 0.331

Note: Hdegoffr = highest degree offered, no degree (0) or associate degree (40); A2224m = completed degree at age 22-24, men; A1819w = completed degree at age 18-19, women; A2021w = completed degree at age 20-21, women.

Figure 7.4 shows the flow of model development for the public institutions with the accepted models highlighted. The figure includes the model number, sector, Pearson's *r* correlation, and the strength of the relationship between the actual and predicted graduation rate. The figure was to place each institution in a peer group by control and level that would result in the highest correlation between the actual and the predicted graduation rate.

After finding that all public and private institutions together in Model 17 did not produce a strong model, the researcher used the control and level variables to segment the data file into Model 14, which contained public and private four-year institutions, and Model 11, which contained public and private two-year and less institutions. Data mining is an explorative process, and the model development continued until the researcher was satisfied with a Pearson's correlation of 0.877 for Model 2, which contained

NEW DIRECTIONS FOR INSTITUTIONAL RESEARCH • DOI: 10.1002/ir

Figure 7.3. Public Four-Year Model Tree

EFTPCTWH ≤ 0.792 [Mode: 3]
  Completers ≤ 182.500 [Mode: 2]
    Igrnt_p ≤ 12 [Mode: 1]
      Stabbr in ["CT" "GU" "NH" "NJ" "NV" "PR"] [Mode: 3]
                                    ≥ 0.347
      Stabbr in ["AL" "DC" "GA" "IL" "IN" "KS" "LA" "MD" "ME" "MN" "MP"
           "NY" "OH" "SD" "TX" "UT" "WV"] Mode: 1]
      Stabbr in ["AL" "LA" "SD" "UT"] [Mode: 1] ≥ 0.097
      Stabbr in ["DC" "GA" "IL" "IN" "KS" "MD" "ME" "MN" "MP" "NY" "OH"
           "TX" "WV"] [Mode: 1] ≥ 0.199
    Igrnt_p > 12 [Mode: 3]
      FyTwom ≤ 998.500 [Mode: 4] ≥ 0.463
      FyTwom >998.500 [Mode: 3]
        E_Ind ≤ 228 [Mode: 3] ≥ 0.326
        E_Ind >228 [Mode: 1] ≥ 0.173
  Completers >182.500 [Mode: 3]
    EFTwom ≤ 834.500 [Mode: 9] ≥ 0.763
    EFTwom >834.500 [Mode: 3]
      Roomcap ≤ 2380.500 [Mode: 3]
        NPEC12 ≤ 54.050 [Mode: 3] ≥ 0.397
        NPEC12 >54.050 [Mode: 3] ≥ 0.32
      Roomcap >2380.500 [Mode: 4]
        SATpct ≤ 82.500 [Mode: 4] ≥ 0.43
        SATpct >82.500 [Mode: 4] ≥ 0.508
EFTPCTWH >0.792 [Mode: 5]
  NPEC18 ≤ 89595 [Mode: 5]
    Avesalm ≤ 52753.500 [Mode: 3] ≥ 0.388
    Avesalm >52753.500 [Mode: 5]
      Ret_pcf ≤ 78.500 [Mode: 5]
        Stabbr in ["CA" "CO" "GA" "HI" "IN" "MI" "MN" "MT" "PA" "TN" "TX"
           "VA"] [Mode: 4] ≥ 0.469
        Stabbr in ["KS" "KY" "MA" "MD" "MS" "NC" "ND" "NH" "NY" "OH"
           "WA" "WI" "WV"] [Mode: 5] ≥ 0.551
      Ret_pcf >78.500 [Mode: 5]
        Enrlptm in ["" "0" "6"] [Mode: 7] ≥ 0.744
        Enrlptm in ["1" "11" "12" "14" "157" "17" "2" "20" "22" "24" "28" "3"
           "4" "43" "5" "58" "9"] [Mode: 5] ≥ 0.606
  NPEC18 >89595 [Mode: 6]
    SATmt75 ≤ 665 [Mode: 6] ≥ 0.668
    SATmt75 >665 [Mode: 8] ≥ 0.799

Note: EFTPCTWH = percentage of full-time enrollment that is white; Igrnt-p = percentage receiving institutional grants; Stabbr = state abbreviations; FyTwom = Full-year unduplicated headcount, women; E_Ind = enrolled, American Indian; EFTwom = enrolled full-time, women; Roomcap = total dormitory capacity; NPEC12 = Percentage of scholarship expenditures from Pell grants; SATpct = Percentage of full-time full-year degree-seeking students submitting SAT scores; NPEC18 = Average faculty salary professor, men; Avesalm = average faculty salary, male; Ret_pcf = full-time retention rate; Enrlptm = enrolled part-time, male; SATmt75 = 75th percentile on SAT math score.

Figure 7.4. Flow of Public Model Development

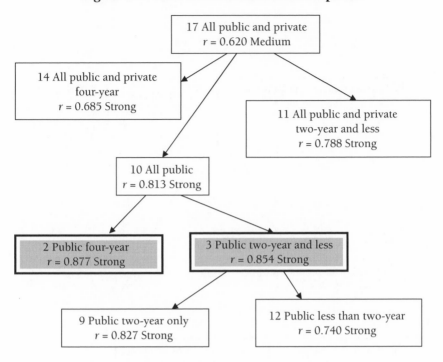

public four-year institutions, and a Pearson's correlation of 0.854 for Model 3, which contained public two-year and less institutions. Segmenting the public two-year and less institutions into two groups resulted in models 9 and 12 with lower r scores, which were rejected. Accepted by the researcher were models 2 and 3.

Figure 7.5 shows the flow of model development for the private institutions with the accepted models highlighted. The private institutions were segmented not only into for-profit and not-for-profit but also by level into four-year, two-year only, and two-year and less. Although all accepted models showed strong correlations between the actual and predicted graduation rates, the Pearson's correlation was lowest at 0.672 for Model 8, which contained the private, for-profit, less than two-year colleges. Accepted by the researcher were models 1, 7, 8, 6, 5, and 4.

In all, twenty-one models were developed for this analysis based on institutional control and level, with eight models being accepted by the researcher and thirteen being rejected. Table 7.6 shows the Pearson's correlation for each of the accepted models. The model with the highest Pearson's correlation of 0.885 is the private for-profit four-year model.

Figure 7.5. Flow of Private Model Development

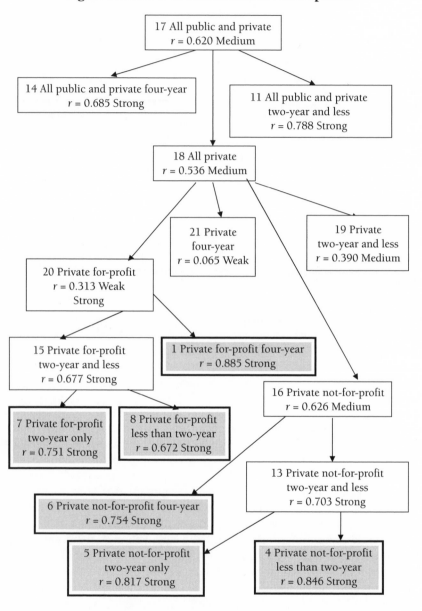

An Example: The Minnesota State System

Currently the Minnesota state system selects peer groups for national graduation rate comparisons using the Carnegie classification code and the degree of urbanization for the public four-year institutions. For the public

**Table 7.6. Models Accepted: Relationship Between Actual
and Predicted Graduation Rate**

Model	Count	Pearson's Correlation r
1. Private for-profit four-year	211	0.885
2. Public four-year	586	0.877
3. Public two-year and less	1,421	0.854
4. Private not-for-profit less than two-year	114	0.846
5. Private not-for-profit two-year only	221	0.817
6. Private not-for-profit four-year	1,273	0.754
7. Private for-profit two-year only	722	0.751
8. Private for-profit less than two-year	1,223	0.672

Note: All correlations are strong.

two-year colleges, peer groups are selected using the degree of urbanization and the percentage of awards in the high-cost program areas of health, trade, and technical fields. The researcher developed peer groups using these variables alone as predictors. The r values for the models developed for this study were 0.877 for the public four-year institutions and 0.854 for the public two-year and less institutions, both showing strong relationships. For models using the current Minnesota system input variables, the Pearson's correlations were 0.603 for the public four-year institutions (medium relationship) and 0.675 for the public two-year institutions (strong). Both of the models developed for this study have r values higher than those produced using only the current Minnesota system input variables of the Carnegie classification code, degree of urbanization, and the percentage of awards in high-cost programs.

In Table 7.7, the actual graduation rates are compared with the weighted predicted graduation rates at Minnesota state system institutions, both four-year and two-year, with a column showing the difference between the two. Each institution was placed in a peer group of similar institutions. A weighted predicted graduation rate was calculated for each peer group. Eighteen of the institutions have actual graduation rates lower than peer group predicted rates, and nineteen of the institutions have actual graduation rates higher than peer group predicted rates.

Implications

This study was undertaken to develop models that help institutional researchers understand IPEDS graduation rates at both two-year and four-year institutions. Predicted graduation rates can provide supplementary information for Student-Right-to-Know disclosure and context for performance measures. When sorted by the predicted graduation rates, similar institutions can be identified for peer analysis. Each institution would be

**Table 7.7. Actual Graduation Rates Compared with
Weighted Predicted Rates**

Minnesota State System Institution	Actual	Predicted	Difference
1. Technical college	0.433	0.689	−0.256
2. Technical college	0.595	0.390	0.205
3. Technical college	0.478	0.310	0.168
4. Community and technical college	0.470	0.310	0.160
5. Community and technical college	0.269	0.390	−0.121
6. Community and technical college	0.246	0.356	−0.110
7. Technical college	0.416	0.310	0.106
8. Community and technical college	0.496	0.390	0.106
9. State university	0.417	0.508	−0.091
10. Technical college	0.269	0.356	−0.087
11. Community and technical college	0.475	0.390	0.085
12. Community college	0.117	0.199	−0.082
13. State university	0.394	0.317	0.077
14. Technical college	0.461	0.390	0.071
15. Community and technical college	0.457	0.390	0.067
16. Community and technical college	0.250	0.310	−0.060
17. Technical college	0.449	0.390	0.059
18. State university	0.534	0.476	0.058
19. Technical college	0.448	0.390	0.058
20. Community college	0.148	0.199	−0.051
21. Community and technical college	0.339	0.390	−0.051
22. Technical college	0.342	0.390	−0.048
23. Community college	0.346	0.390	−0.044
24. Community and technical college	0.161	0.199	−0.038
25. Community and technical college	0.428	0.390	0.038
26. Technical college	0.418	0.390	0.028
27. State university	0.499	0.476	0.023
28. Community college	0.112	0.094	0.018
29. Community college	0.182	0.199	−0.017
30. State university	0.459	0.476	−0.017
31. State university	0.377	0.390	−0.013
32. State university	0.184	0.196	−0.012
33. Community and technical college	0.208	0.199	0.009
34. Community college	0.205	0.196	0.009
35. Community and technical college	0.384	0.390	−0.006
36. Community college	0.360	0.356	0.004
37. Community and technical college	0.091	0.094	−0.003

placed into similar peer groups for comparing graduation rates because the predicted graduated rate is the weighted average graduation rate for all the institutions in the peer group.

Of the postsecondary institutional research literature available in the United States, this data-mining study may be the first to use one data source and one method to produce predicted graduation rates for postsecondary institutions in every sector and level. This study is significant in several ways. First, most existing research related to graduation rates seeks to explain student behavior or to identify factors leading to retention or degree attainment at the student level. This study is done at the institutional level using aggregate data to provide national comparisons.

Second, federal and state policymakers view graduation rates as an indication of performance at both two-year and four-year postsecondary institutions. No research currently in the literature uses data-mining techniques on IPEDS data to explain graduation rates at both two- and four-year institutions.

Third, two-year colleges in the United States are diverse. Little research has been done examining graduation rates of two-year colleges using IPEDS data.

Finally, the Minnesota State Colleges and Universities is a complex system of two-year colleges and four-year universities. Few researchers use data-mining techniques to analyze such a diverse system.

References

Astin, A. "College Retention Rates Are Often Misleading." *Chronicle of Higher Education,* 1993. http://chronicle.com/che-data/articles.dir/articles-40.dir/issue05.dir/05a04801. htm. Accessed Aug. 27, 2005.

Luan, J. "Data Mining and Its Applications in Higher Education." In A. M. Serban and J. Luan (eds.), *Knowledge Management: Building a Competitive Advantage in Higher Education.* New Directions for Institutional Research, no. 113. San Francisco: Jossey-Bass, 2002.

The Measurement Group. "CART or C&RT." 1999. http://www.themeasurementgroup. com/Definitions/CART.htm. Accessed Dec. 5, 2005.

National Center for Education Statistics. "IPEDS Glossary." 2000. http://nces.ed.gov/ ipeds/glossary/index.asp?id=447. Accessed Sept. 5, 2006.

National Center for Education Statistics. *Classification of Instructional Programs: 2000 Edition* (NCES 2002-165). Washington, D.C.: U.S. Department of Education, 2002.

National Postsecondary Education Cooperative. "NPEC IPEDS Data Feedback Report: 2004." http://nces.ed.gov/npec/datafeedback.asp. Accessed July 21, 2005.

Schuh, J. "The Integrated Postsecondary Education Data System." In B. E. Bender and J. H. Schuh, *Using Benchmarking to Inform Practice in Higher Education.* New Directions for Higher Education, no. 118. San Francisco: Jossey-Bass, 2002.

StatSoft, Inc. "Classification and Regression Trees (C&RT)." 1984. http://www.statsoft. com/textbook/stcart.html. Accessed Dec. 5, 2005.

Student Right-to-Know and Campus Security Act. Public Law 101-542. Washington, D.C: 101st Congress, Second Session, 1990.

Brenda L. Bailey is associate director for research at the Minnesota State Colleges and Universities, a system that contains public two-year and four-year institutions.

New Directions for Institutional Research • DOI: 10.1002/ir

8

As a tour de force, data mining is likely to gain wider use in the next few years. To facilitate this transition, we make several recommendations addressed to both institutional research professionals and the Association of Institutional Research.

Practicing Data Mining for Enrollment Management and Beyond

Jing Luan, Chun-Mei Zhao

Institutional researchers often feel frustrated as assumptions for valid statistical inferences are often violated when dealing with real institutional research problems and when messy, ambiguous, and incomplete data are present. Data mining, in contrast to the traditional experimental study rationale, seeks specific and unique patterns within granular data records—the smallest units of analysis. It is foremost a practical application and by nature an iterative process. Its processes lead to models that provide actionable information. In this sense, data mining is increasingly useful and particularly fitting for institutional research tasks.

It is not easy to transcribe data mining's iterative model development processes into scholarly chapters as one would expect researchers to do with their traditional statistical studies. Nevertheless, the authors in this volume took the time to describe their work in as detailed a manner as possible to give readers a glimpse of how data mining can be applied to problems challenging today's institutional researchers.

These case studies indicate that data mining can be applied to enrollment management with ease. In several cases, data-mining approaches helped shed new light on previously well-researched topics as well as broke new ground. They demonstrated data mining's flexibility in adapting to various databases, large and small, and at various data aggregation levels. As shown, data mining is a desirable addition to enrollment management, in particular, and to institutional research in general.

NEW DIRECTIONS FOR INSTITUTIONAL RESEARCH, no. 131, Fall 2006   © Wiley Periodicals, Inc.
Published online in Wiley InterScience (www.interscience.wiley.com) • DOI: 10.1002/ir.191

Data mining is a comprehensive process with well-established procedures called CRISP-DM. The business world has long benefited from these standard procedures. Data mining almost forces one to conduct thorough work from the start of collecting data all the way to the final scoring. All of the authors have documented the results of their work right before live scoring.

As we pointed out in Chapter One and exemplified by the case studies, data mining does not exclude the use of traditional statistics but, rather, the two approaches complement each other. The arrival of data mining has simply made more tools available for researchers. Data mining is quite capable of conducting traditional statistical tasks, which helps researchers understand and explain the results produced by other more sophisticated algorithms. For instance, in Chapter Six, the author employed both traditional statistical tests and modern data-mining algorithms to understand University of California students' use of advanced-placement units to shorten their time in college.

However, there are differences between data mining and traditional statistics, of which many researchers have not become thoroughly aware. Researchers wonder how to approach data analysis without the guidance of theories, hypotheses, and tests of significance. These have been the essential staples of inferential statistics, much the same as physicians have relied on stethoscopes and x-ray machines. And yet, just as doctors have come to rely on new technologies to obtain faster and more accurate and individualized diagnoses, researchers should embrace tested and proven new approaches to data analysis.

In many situations, data mining has distinct advantages over the conventional analytical approaches. It is a powerful tool in implementing effective student interventions previously not often practiced, particularly in predicting and scoring behaviors of individual students. For instance, the case studies in chapters four and five showed that data mining allowed the universities under study to obtain a list of students who were believed to soon drop out. This allowed the universities to gain valuable time and take preemptive measures.

Theories developed in the past decades concerning students' retention, as readers have come to notice in the case studies, served to guide researchers in identifying data sources and understanding interactions of data elements. After that, data mining goes beyond to fully explore the data and return highly diverse multiple rules and patterns governing individual students' behaviors. Data mining is keen on individual differences. Luan (2005) illustrated the difference between the conventional statistical approach to the treatment of variables and that of data mining. He argued that every variable is of significance to particular individual cases if one is to obtain the pinpoint accuracy of prediction in data mining. The practice of reducing the number of variables is discouraged in data mining because even though some variables may have little significance to the overall prediction outcome, they can be essential to a specific record.

To test a data set with multiple algorithms is a fundamental principle in scientific data analysis. How would a scientific theory or discovery be valid if it is not devoid of method bias and not replicable? To whit, many research published reports still contain results and even theorizing and generalizing about a model based on one statistical test alone. It is common knowledge, however, that just about every algorithm will produce a different result set! In this volume, multiple algorithms were applied in several case studies to test models to ensure that algorithmic bias (method bias) has been examined and the algorithm with the best prediction accuracy is selected to be the final model. What is also worth emphasizing is the data-mining approach of identifying both a training and validation data set. The use of training and validation data sets serves as an empirical way of guaranteeing the accuracy of any "scoring" done by the final data-mining model.

Looking ahead, we believe strongly that the era of data mining is upon us. For a new tool or approach to be accepted, many obstacles must be overcome. For example, the process for accepting data mining by the field of practice in higher education involved writing white papers, conducting product demonstrations, hosting workshops, and identifying early adopters of this technology. The Association of Institutional Research (AIR) has been a pioneer in working with us to explore the potential of data mining. For several years, data-mining workshops have been held at the AIR annual forums and during regional conferences. Hundreds of institutional researchers have been trained in data-mining techniques, and many of them have installed data-mining applications developed by different vendors such as SPSS [Statistical Package for the Social Sciences], Inc. A special-interest group was formed and received unwavering support from AIR. Since the late 1990s, data mining has been gradually introduced to the institutional researchers and decision makers in higher education institutions. All in all, a critical mass of knowledge base and users is emerging.

To ensure the success of fully adopting data-mining technology and applications, more work is ahead of us. As editors of this volume, we would like to put forward two sets of recommendations. One is for institutional researchers, faculty, and staff who are potential users and beneficiaries of data mining, and the other is for AIR.

Recommendations for Institutional Research Professionals

• *Explore the power of real-time database scoring.* We strongly suggest that data-mining models, once finalized, be deployed over live data warehouses to score the data in real time.

Rationale: Most data-mining activities, as indicated by published articles and the case studies reported in this volume, have stopped before the last, and yet the most useful, step of live scoring. This is largely because the data warehouse technology currently avails itself only as a one-way street, meaning that the researchers can obtain the data for analysis but are unable to write back. Being able to deploy a data-mining model over a live database, much the same way as any number of applications that interface with Banner, SAP, Peoplesoft, or Datatel, would provide the most business advantage. The phrase "knowledge discovery in databases" is meant to express the task of scoring the data using a data-mining model in a live database so that decision makers can obtain results in real time.

• *Adopt algorithmic bias analysis.* We strongly suggest that institutional researchers adopt the use of multiple algorithms to compare results. This also implies the use of a training data set and at least one validation data set for conducting algorithmic bias analysis.

Rationale: We have been arguing against the inadequate practice by scholars in examining and reporting the results based on one statistical test. In many cases, at least two or more statistical tests are needed to make sure the results are free from the bias of the test itself. It is a documented fact that, as noted in the chapters of this book, results may vary and, at times, highly vary from test to test. To rely on results from one test (algorithm) alone to draw conclusions that affect the decisions made by an institution or even larger organizational body is unscientific. The impact on the lives of students as a result is worth serious consideration to stop that practice.

Closely related to this is the use of training plus validation data sets to examine the accuracy of any model. Significance tests, though useful for a number of applications such as test-retest of group means analysis, have lost their relevance in data mining where significance is defined as the accuracy of predicting the outcome for a case. Because the unit of analysis is increasingly granular, and individualized pattern recognition and treatment for students are considered far superior over the traditional broad theories, scholars will find the use of multiple mirrored data sets as a better way of testing for significance.

• *Explore the use of cluster analysis, association, and visualization.* We strongly suggest that institutional researchers conduct "unsupervised" data-mining analysis with visualization, association, and cluster analysis being the key components.

Rationale: The existing training of statistics both on the job and in the graduate curriculum covers very briefly the subjects of cluster analysis, including factor analysis and association rules. Cluster analysis is increasingly useful when dealing with large data sets and particularly helpful in identifying outliers. When used before predictive modeling, cluster analysis helps with understanding the data and reducing the data into meaningful and manageable parts. In addition, data visualization has remained stagnant at the level of basic charts while unable to be treated as another way of expressing data (the other way being mathematical symbols and equations) (Tufte, 2001).

NEW DIRECTIONS FOR INSTITUTIONAL RESEARCH • DOI: 10.1002/ir

- *Explore the use of data mining in all facets of research, including text mining.* Last, we strongly suggest that data mining be applied beyond enrollment management and beyond being strictly codified and numerical. This means that researchers may attempt to use data mining for almost all research activities that are above management reporting and to include text mining.

Rationale: Data mining for enrollment management, as demonstrated by the case studies in this book, has provided the feasibility and evidence for data mining to be applied in many more aspects of institutional research. Enrollment management is a central and core activity of a higher education institution; therefore, what is good for enrollment management may well be just as appropriate for other research tasks. Outside the field of higher education, data mining has proved to be a core business application for marketing, customer retention ("churn rate"), and credit risk, among others. The use of data mining by the government in sifting through personal records, codified or text based, although controversial, helps reinforce the notion that data mining has tremendous business and educational value and has gone beyond being an alternative to traditional statistical analysis to become the mainstay of modern institutional research.

Recommendations for AIR

- *Develop a regular data-mining training course.* It is recommended that AIR work with current data-mining faculty and users to design a training course and incorporate such a course as part of its regular technology institute curriculum.

Rationale: Currently there is no formal presence of data mining as a course in the technology institute provided by AIR. To make it part of any of the institutes would give data mining the official stamp of approval and will greatly enhance its rate of adoption.

- *Work with vendors to reduce costs.* It is recommended that AIR work with well-established vendors, such as SPSS and SAS [Statistical Analysis System] Institute, Inc., to explore the possibility of group discounts for data-mining software.

Rationale: Currently the pricing is one of the major concerns of the users, and it varies depending on when it is asked and of whom.

- *Provide grant support for Data Mining in Higher Education (DMHE) consortium.* It is recommended that the organizers of the DMHE consortium work with the AIR grant committee to develop grant proposals for supporting small-scale data-mining research activities.

Rationale: Formed on May 16, 2006, the DMHE is the clearinghouse of data mining in institutional research and the organization representing researchers who conduct data mining. This fledgling entity needs seed money and support in the forms of volunteers and other generous donations to achieve its mission.

New Directions for Institutional Research • DOI: 10.1002/ir

References

Luan, J. "Moving Beyond the Basics: Get an Edge in Institutional Research with Data Mining." SPSS/AIR Professional Development Webinar Series, Dec. 12, 2005. http://www.spss.com/airseries. Accessed Sept. 18, 2006.

Tufte, E. *The Visual Display of Quantitative Information.* Cheshire, Conn.: Graphic Press, 2001.

JING LUAN is vice chancellor of Educational Services and Planning at San Mateo Community College District in California.

CHUN-MEI ZHAO is research scholar, the Carnegie Foundation for the Advancement of Teaching.

NEW DIRECTIONS FOR INSTITUTIONAL RESEARCH • DOI: 10.1002/ir

INDEX

Back Issue/Subscription Order Form

Copy or detach and send to:

Jossey-Bass, A Wiley Imprint, 989 Market Street, San Francisco CA 94103-1741

Call or fax toll-free: Phone 888-378-2537 6:30AM – 3PM PST; Fax 888-481-2665

Back Issues: Please send me the following issues at $29 each

(Important: please include ISBN number for each issue.)

_____

_____

_____

$ _____   Total for single issues

$ _____   SHIPPING CHARGES: SURFACE   Domestic Canadian
                                            First Item $5.00 $6.00
                                            Each Add'l Item $3.00 $1.50
                 For next-day and second-day delivery rates, call the number listed above.

Subscriptions   Please __ start __ renew my subscription to *New Directions for Institutional Research* for the year 2_____at the following rate:

U.S.   __ Individual $80   __ Institutional $185

Canada   __ Individual $80   __ Institutional $225

All Others   __ Individual $104   __ Institutional $269

Online subscriptions are available via Wiley InterScience!

**For more information about online subscriptions visit
www.wileyinterscience.com**

$ _____   Total single issues and subscriptions (Add appropriate sales tax for your state for single issue orders. No sales tax for U.S. subscriptions. Canadian residents, add GST for subscriptions and single issues.)

__Payment enclosed (U.S. check or money order only)

__VISA __ MC __ AmEx # _____ Exp. Date _____

Signature _____ Day Phone _____

__ Bill Me (U.S. institutional orders only. Purchase order required.)

Purchase order # _____
                    Federal Tax ID13559302   **GST 89102 8052**

Name _____

Address _____

_____

Phone _____ E-mail _____

For more information about Jossey-Bass, visit our Web site at www.josseybass.com

demands of state officials, accrediting agencies, employers, prospective students, parents, and the general public.
ISBN: 0-7879-8228-8

IR125   **Minority Retention: What Works?**
Gerald H. Gaither
Examines some of the best policies, practices, and procedures to achieve greater diversity and access, while controlling costs and maintaining quality. Looks at institutions that are majority-serving, tribal, Hispanic-serving, and historically black. Emphasizes that the key to retention is in the professional commitment of faculty and staff to student-centered efforts, and includes practical ideas adaptable to different institutional goals.
ISBN: 0-7879-7974-0

IR124   **Unique Campus Contexts: Insights for Research and Assessment**
Jason E. Lane, M. Christopher Brown II
Summarizes what we know about professional schools, transnational campuses, proprietary schools, religious institutions, and corporate universities. As more students take advantage of these specialized educational environments, conducting meaningful research becomes a challenge. The authors argue for the importance of educational context and debunk the one-size-fits-all approach to assessment, evaluation, and research. Effective institutional measures of inquiry, benchmarks, and indicators must be congruent with the mission, population, and function of each unique campus context.
ISBN: 0-7879-7973-2

IR123   **Successful Strategic Planning**
Michael J. Dooris, John M. Kelley, James F. Trainer
Explains the value of strategic planning in higher education to improve conditions and meet missions (hiring better faculty, recruiting stronger students, upgrading facilities, improving programs, acquiring resources), and what planning tools and methodologies have been used at various campuses. Goes beyond the activity of planning to investigate successful ways to implement and infuse strategic plans throughout the organization. Case studies from various campuses show different ways to achieve success.
ISBN: 0-7879-7792-6

IR122   **Assessing Character Outcomes in College**
Jon C. Dalton, Terrence R. Russell, Sally Kline
Examines several perspectives on the role of higher education in developing students' character, and illustrates approaches to defining and assessing character outcomes. Moral, civic, ethical, and spiritual development are key aspects of students' growth and experience in college, so how can educators encourage good values and assess their impact?
ISBN: 0-7879-7791-8

IR121   **Overcoming Survey Research Problems**
Stephen R. Porter
As demand for survey research has increased, survey response rates have decreased. This volume examines an array of survey research problems and best practices, from both the literature and field practitioners, to provide solutions to increase response rates while controlling costs. Discusses administering longitudinal studies, doing surveys on sensitive topics such as student drug and alcohol use, and using new technologies for survey administration.
ISBN: 0-7879-7477-3

IR120   **Using Geographic Information Systems in Institutional Research**
Daniel Teodorescu
Exploring the potential of geographic information systems (GIS) applications
in higher education administration, this issue introduces IR professionals and
campus administrators to a powerful presentation and analysis tool. Chapters
explore the benefits of working with the spatial component of data in
recruitment, admissions, facilities, alumni development, and other areas, with
examples of actual GIS applications from several higher education institutions.
ISBN: 0-7879-7281-9

IR119   **Maximizing Revenue in Higher Education**
F. King Alexander, Ronald G. Ehrenberg
This volume presents edited versions of some of the best articles from a forum
on institutional revenue generation sponsored by the Cornell Higher Education
Research Institute. The chapters provide different perspectives on revenue
generation and how institutions are struggling to find an appropriate balance
between meeting public expectations and maximizing private market forces.
The insights provided about options and alternatives will enable campus
leaders, institutional researchers, and policymakers to better understand
evolving patterns in public and private revenue reliance.
ISBN: 0-7879-7221-5

IR118   **Studying Diverse Institutions: Contexts, Challenges, and Considerations**
M. Christopher Brown II, Jason E. Lane
This volume examines the contextual and methodological issues pertaining to
studying diverse institutions (including women's colleges, tribal colleges, and
military academies), and provides effective and useful approaches for higher
education administrators, institutional researchers and planners, policymakers,
and faculty seeking to better understand students in postsecondary education.
It also offers guidelines to asking the right research questions, employing the
appropriate research design and methods, and analyzing the data with respect
to the unique institutional contexts.
ISBN: 0-7879-6990-7

IR117   **Unresolved Issues in Conducting Salary-Equity Studies**
Robert K. Toutkoushian
Chapters discuss the issues surrounding how to use faculty rank, seniority, and
experience as control variables in salary-equity studies. Contributors review the
challenges of conducting a salary-equity study for nonfaculty administrators
and staff—who constitute the majority of employees, even in academic
institutions—and examine the advantages and disadvantages of using
hierarchical linear modeling to measure pay equity. They present a case-study
approach to illustrate the political and practical challenges that researchers
often face when conducting a salary-equity study for an institution. This is a
companion volume to *Conducting Salary-Equity Studies: Alternative Approaches
to Research* (IR115).
ISBN: 0-7879-6863-3